Also by Jason Makansi

*Painting By Numbers: How to Sharpen
Your BS Detector and Smoke Out the Experts*

*Lights Out: The Electricity Crisis,
The Global Economy, and What it Means to You*

*An Investor's Guide to the Electricity Economy*

*The Moment Before: A Novel*

# Carbon IRA & YouTility

How to Address Climate Change
& Reward Carbon Reduction
Before It's Too Late

*by*

## JASON MAKANSI

Layla Dog Press | Tucson, AZ

For information, contact layladogpress@gmail.com

Manufactured in the United States of America
Publication date: October 1, 2019
Cover Design by Kristina Blank Makansi
Interior Illustrations by Elena K. Makansi
Cover Art: Shutterstock
Library of Congress Control Number:  2019902895
ISBN:  9780998425924

To all the good people in the electricity industry
who keep the lights on and the AC system humming,
the machines whirring, and devices charging.
Thank you for your dedication to making electricity
available to almost everyone. Now it's time to undertake
the next challenge—making our industry carbon friendly
and climate neutral in the shortest time frame possible.

# CONTENTS

# PREFACE

According to the 2018 Intergovernmental Panel on Climate Change (IPCC) report from the most expert of experts (91 of them from forty countries) in climate modeling and climate change, adverse human impacts on global climate are worsening. Under present conditions, we have twelve years before the planet changes irreparably, potentially harming tens of millions of people.

We are on our way, these scientists say, to an average two degree C rise in global temperatures by 2030, the threshold for the most severe impacts on the planet.

We have to act. Fast.

Nominally, 55-60 percent of the carbon build-up from humans comes from electricity and transportation. If we wish to respond and address climate change swiftly, we don't need to look any further than these two sectors.

Figure 1. Transportation and electricity account for the largest share of carbon emissions

Most people consume electricity, and everyone needs to get from one place to another. Yet one billion people on this planet don't have ready access to electricity! It's a safe bet that they would like to enjoy the benefits of electricity, too, as well as motorized transportation.

Ironically, *more* electricity, but from carbon-free sources, is the quickest way to address our crisis.

The good news is that the electricity industry, at least in the developed countries, is on the cusp of the necessary transformation to a low-carbon future. The bad news is that it's been on the cusp for too many years.

I've enjoyed a 40-year career in the electricity industry, and most of those years were spent following and analyzing regulatory and technological trends and developments. After receiving my BS in chemical engineering from Columbia University in the City of New York, I went to work for the Tennessee Valley Authority, following a summer paid internship program between junior and senior years. I worked in a group developing new emissions testing methods and protocols. I spent only a year at TVA, but I worked on-site at many of the coal-fired plants and one gas-fired turbine plant.

Then I returned to NYC and took a job with a small engineering firm, and spent two years mostly working at a refinery in New Jersey, also on environmental projects. After that, I landed my dream job as an editor for a prominent engineering trade publication serving the electric power generation sector. For the next eighteen years, I would function as an analyst, visiting facilities and evaluating virtually every new technology relevant to electricity generation. We launched an international version of the magazine, and several spinoffs. We created a web-based news service ten years before people started reading the news on their computers and phones. And one of my responsibilities was to help select the winners of our annual plant technology awards.

In this capacity, I wrote about the first significantly-sized solar PV installation in the early 1980s, visited the largest wind turbine in Europe in the early 1990s, awarded to the largest grid-scale energy storage facility (not a battery!) our plant technology prize in the mid-1990s, and evaluated the world's largest advanced battery facilities. I've witnessed the rise and fall and consolidation of companies, several industry booms and busts, and many sector booms and busts within the industry.

In short, I've followed intimately how new technology disrupts the industry, suffers through and overcomes setbacks, and ultimately prevails if it is truly better and can scale to the commercial needs of a huge, critical service like electricity.

Therefore, the judgments and conclusions I make in this book are based on four decades of experience analyzing the delicate dance among technology, policy, politics, and business in the electricity industry, as well as its rich history and role in the nation's economy.

And I know that to accomplish the change necessary to stave off the ravages of a warmer planet within the next twelve years, we need to give transformation of the electricity industry a shove.

Fortunately, we don't need to wait on any technology development. All the technology and products needed for this transformation are available commercially, even if some are more mature than others, as I explain in later chapters.

We do need to quit arguing about the severity of climate change, quit posturing over who's going to make the most money, mute the climate deniers, motivate consumers to make necessary behavior modifications, and motivate producers to rapidly replace our existing electricity delivery system with one based on no- or low-carbon infrastructure.

The ideas presented in this book represent a quick-start way forward. If we organize the electricity industry around two core principles—the Carbon IRA and the YouTility—we may yet be able to stave off disaster.

The Carbon IRA is a way to motivate electricity consumers to use less and get engaged with solutions for individuals. The YouTility is a way to accelerate the infrastructure transformation on the production and delivery side.

The Carbon IRA is libertarian in nature: incentivize and educate people to make better choices rather than conscript them into doing so. This should help overcome the liberal/progressive-conservative/market chasm that infects our politics. Similarly, the YouTility also expands on a well-established economic and business framework: the regulated utility.

We need to establish a virtuous feedback loop: Suppliers of low- or no-carbon solutions will respond to motivated consumers choosing these options. This sets in motion the classic principle of market economics—higher demand, more production and competition, lower costs.

If this book is at all successful, you will be compelled to seek out and have a conversation with your utility, your public utility commission (PUC) representatives, your landlord, your neighborhood association, your car dealership, and your friends and family. It will compel you to search *within* for ways to reduce your *own*, individual carbon footprint, rather than waiting for your elected officials or utility to act with appropriate haste.

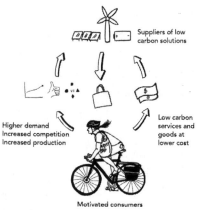

Figure 2. A virtuous feedback loop for reducing carbon emissions.

If we're going to address this crisis in twelve years, every American will need to actively engage with and take responsibility for his or her electricity consumption and modes of transportation.

At the electricity industry's largest annual conference ten years ago, I heard a utility executive say he hoped that within twelve months no one would be talking about electricity. "We operate best when electricity is in the background," he said. *But that is exactly the wrong attitude.* (Fortunately, fewer utility executives would say that today.) I want everyone to talk about electricity, and to take responsibility and do their part in the coming transformation.

I'm not talking about phasing out electricity or crippling the industry for some elusive global environmental goal. No one who truly knows anything about the industry is suggesting modern civilization needs to turn back the clock. Far from it. I'm talking about racing the climate change doomsday clock by *expanding* the electricity industry. I'm talking about transforming the industry from a primary *cause* of climate change to the fundamental *solution* for addressing climate change now.

With urgency.

Before it's too late.

Before you read on, understand that this book is not about the science of human-induced climate change. If you want to continue that debate, take it elsewhere. It's an important debate to have, unless you are a straight up climate science denier, in which case you have deeper issues with how scientific knowledge is constructed, not climate change, per se.

This book accepts the urgency of the latest reports, signed onto by the vast majority of climatologists.

## UNINTENDED CONSEQUENCES

But while this book accepts the legitimacy and urgency of the latest reports, it also recognizes that every broadly applied technology has unintended consequences, often on a large scale. Remember that the automobile in the early part of the last century was considered a great solution to the plague of horse manure in the cities. Now the $CO_2$-spewing gasoline-powered auto, en masse, is the second largest contributor to climate change.

Some of the technologies advocated for in this book may have similar unanticipated and unintended consequences. Lithium-ion batteries, for example, are sure to cause environmental impact from lithium mining, importing and exporting, and reuse at the end of battery life (just like auto batteries today). Fires and explosions are a continuing source of risk with lithium-based (and other types) batteries, especially at large scale.

And many of the "system components" for implementing the concepts I describe rely on digital technology. Each day, it seems, we discover that digital technology poses more security and privacy issues that must be recognized and grappled with.

It is critical that industry identify and confront these consequences and plan now to mitigate them. Something like 90+ percent of lead from lead acid batteries is recycled today. Hopefully, we've gotten a little smarter and are better able to think and plan ahead as an industrial society than we have in the past. Our future depends on it.

## THE TIMELINE

Finally, the book assumes that the twelve-year timeline of the latest IPCC report is real. While some may believe it to be a bit melodramatic, it never hurts to mitigate a threat sooner rather than later. Therefore, the concepts in this book address the question: *What is the fastest way to make the most progress in twelve years?*

# CARBON IRA

# PART I

# INTRODUCTION

In 2007, my well-reviewed and highly regarded book, *Lights Out: The Electricity Crisis, the Global Economy, and What It Means To You,* was published. Much of it is out of date now. Some of it was out of date shortly after it was first released. Such is the nature of books on current events.

For a professional industry book, however, it sold quite well. The electricity industry was in a state of mild crisis and people were more than mildly interested. The crisis was largely induced by abnormally high electricity and energy prices, and pocketbook issues tend to animate the electorate—and readers.

I wrote the last chapter of the book as a bit of a rant. I remember being consumed by the words I put to paper. My head got hot as I typed them. But alas, it would be another several years before I could articulate even to myself how to convert that rant into a program that could actually be implemented.

It took ten years, in fact, to convert that chapter from something like a zealot on a soapbox in the park, hollering at passersby, to a rational framework cogently argued by an industry expert.

This book is that rational framework. This time, the crisis is severe and the timeline short. It's not a crisis of the pocketbook. It's a humanitarian crisis. It's an existential crisis. It's the "challenge" looming behind the scenes when I wrote *Lights Out*. It was the

Figure 3. A man, his message, and his soapbox

big wave far out to sea, threatening to come ashore, but since few could "see it," no one acted with any urgency.

Now, that wave is crashing ashore like a giant tsunami.

At the time of *Lights Out*, the electricity industry was dealing with more immediate crises—those of grid reliability, historically high energy prices, and global terrorist threats. Shortly after the book came out, the

"Great Recession" hit, which eclipsed all of the other crises America faced at that time.

The *challenge* looming offstage then was climate change. Now that challenge is a full-fledged global *crisis*. Hundreds of the most respected climate scientists from around the world recently issued a report forecasting dire disruptions around the globe resulting from climate warming as early as 2030. We are already seeing the early symptoms in more frequent, more extreme, and often catastrophic weather events.

The rant I was on in the last chapter of *Lights Out* was about two things:

1. lack of consumer engagement with their electricity use,
2. lack of innovation in the electricity industry.

I'm happy to report that at least the second of these has been addressed. Considerable time and money—both public and private—has been invested in the research, development, and demonstration of the technologies necessary to transform the electricity industry from one of the primary global climate change problems to one of the primary global climate change solutions. Now, we just need to get busy building out these new systems, quickly phase out the obsolete ones, and embrace a modern paradigm for the next century.

Sadly, we have not made nearly as much progress on consumer engagement with electricity use. Even people deeply troubled by the threat of global climate disruptions tend to wring their hands rather than "get them dirty" taking the steps necessary to contribute to the solution.

This book addresses these two issues as pillars on which we can build a better electricity future:

1.  Incentivize consumers, especially young ones, to change their behavior permanently,
2.  Build out the new electricity infrastructure *with the urgency commensurate with the global climate change crisis we all face.*

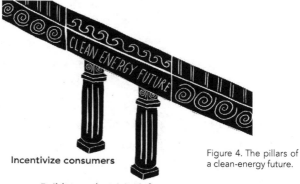

Figure 4. The pillars of a clean-energy future.

Incentivize consumers

Build new electricity infrastructure

I call this book a manifesto or a call to arms (figuratively speaking!). While there are promising changes taking place in the electricity industry that will lead to a far lower carbon intensity in the decades ahead, the pace of that change is still well behind the rate of adverse climate impact.

Generally, you don't propose sweeping new ideas because you think society is going to adopt them lock, stock, and barrel. You propose them to get people thinking in different ways in the hope that perhaps some aspects of the ideas will be adopted over time. Unfortunately, we don't have the luxury of "over time." Our crisis is upon us, and we need to take action now.

## THE UNIFIED FIELD FRAMEWORK

I call the two halves of this little volume a "unified field framework." Like physicists trying to unify the fundamental forces—gravity, electromagnetic, strong, and weak—under one explanatory theory, I'm trying to re-align (or unify) the behavior of electricity consumers and producers to create a classic economic feedback loop: higher demand, more production and competition, and lower costs.

Win, win, win.

The big idea in Part I of this book and the slightly less big idea in Part II work together like a double helix. My hope is that as a "unified field framework" they will accelerate the overhaul of the electricity industry. It is long, *long* overdue. Now, the climate science tells us we have twelve years.

Figure 5. The DNA, or "unified field framework" of Carbon IRA & YouTility.

The BIG idea, the Carbon Individual Retirement Account (Carbon IRA) is truly novel. The electricity industry has been in the crosshairs of the global climate change debate for decades. I've been writing about and consulting in that industry for forty years. I've done the research. And I have not found any other proposition describing the coupling of behavioral changes to reduce carbon footprint with a long-term retirement savings plan.

This is the incentive. This is the reward, long-term.

This is also a solution to the problem of insufficient savings among younger workers grappling with college debt and facing a future affected by climate change.

The less-big idea, the YouTility, is a unique way of talking about what is already happening in the electricity industry, just far too slowly.

It's a way of branding the transition from a centralized command and control electricity industry ("we supply it, you buy it, it's vanilla…") to a distributed two-way system in which every consumer can also be a supplier and/or an active, engaged consumer of electricity rather than a passive buyer and waster of electricity.

This is the action.

Simply, the Carbon IRA provides the incentive for an electricity consumer to begin acting like a YouTility, someone who takes responsibility and control of his or her electricity consumption *and* the carbon associated with it.

The asymptotic limit of this double helix framework is someone who is not only drastically reducing his or her electricity costs, and perhaps even selling excess electricity to the "grid," but someone who is drastically reducing his or her individual carbon footprint *and being rewarded for it with deposits in a retirement account!*

The economic consequences of this framework are almost inconceivable. Almost everything about energy economics will be upended. Almost everything about the policy and business institutions that essentially control how the electricity industry evolves will be upended, too.

The beauty of this unifying framework is that it is a bottoms-up strategy. It doesn't have to be driven by command and control government regulation, although regulation could accelerate it. And it doesn't rely on incremental changes to the existing market structure which has traditionally constrained innovation in the electricity industry or by environmental organization stakeholders.

The unifying framework gets at the heart of what drives real change, empowering people to make decisions on their own behalf. This is especially important in a market-oriented economy like ours which, despite current political debate, is not going to change anytime soon.

There is no shortage of experts and stakeholders telling you how to "be part of the solution" to climate change and how you can be a better electricity consumer. Most of these well-reasoned and intentioned suggestions come with a great deal of complicated language and jargon.

Electricity supply and consumption *is* complicated. Each benefit seems to be counter-balanced with a disadvantage. Entrenched interests on *all* sides of the debate resist disruption. After all, no matter which side of the debate you're on, you have jobs to do, money to make, families to raise, and policy prescriptions and business models that have been refined over many decades.

Some advocate imposing a carbon tax on business, some want to stick it to the big fossil fuel companies, and others want higher efficiency in all systems because they think that will make the problem go away.

The Carbon IRA & YouTility unifying framework is something that, I hope, makes all of them seriously uncomfortable. Why? Because converting electricity from the problem to the solution doesn't have to be as complicated as most people make it out to be.

The fact is that everything that I propose in these pages can be implemented now. We don't need entrepreneurs to invent new things. We don't need policy wonks or Beltway bandits to write new position papers. We don't need new government regulations. All the elements of Carbon IRA and YouTility are either commercially available today, or can be adapted from other contexts and sectors.

What we *do* need are consumers to demand a new long-term incentive structure and to make decisions based on these new incentives. Industry stakeholders will respond to those decisions and companies will offer products and services that accommodate them.

We also need carbon-enlightened companies to make some relatively minor adjustments to programs they are already implementing. I say "minor adjustments" because the only new things required to implement a Carbon

IRA-YouTility framework is new thinking and collective will.

There's nothing new in accounting for carbon reductions ($CO_2$ equivalent) of different behaviors and consumer choices, in converting that carbon into financial value, or in setting up and managing a retirement fund. You just have to integrate these pieces into a unified program. And, there's nothing new about encouraging an electricity consumer to rely on new "smart" thermostats, add solar photovoltaics (PV) and home energy storage

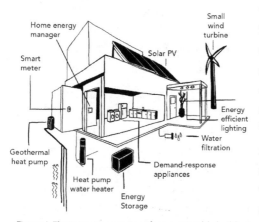

Figure 6. There are many options for a sustainable building

to the energy infrastructure of the home or business, choose energy-efficient appliances, and drive an electric vehicle.

But the range of options available to a home or business owner to become an active engaged consumer is far higher than any utility or government incentive program is willing to include.

This is where I want the entrenched interests to get seriously uncomfortable. I want regulated utilities to see that thousands of "YouTilities" in their service territory threaten their core business model. I want that to be so uncomfortable that they realize their best response is to encourage every consumer to *become* a YouTility and help them achieve their goals and aspirations or to supply zero-carbon electricity themselves and phase out fossil fuels. That way, the utility continues to pursue its core business model rather than sees YouTility as an existential threat.

This isn't about putting utilities out of business. Unless, that is, they fail to respond to their customers, in which case they deserve to go out of business. Instead, it's about accelerating the transformation already taking place, but far, *far* too slowly.

I want environmental advocacy and policy organizations to see that the Carbon IRA idea threatens all of the policy frameworks they have previously proposed.

Nobody "required" consumers to prefer cellphones and ultimately give up landlines. The benefits were so compelling that this happened organically. Likewise, nobody "decided" that mainframe computers should become obsolete. The PC, then the laptop, then personal digital devices, all offered such compelling advantages that this transition also occurred organically.

Now, we have an opportunity to transform the electricity grid, drastically reduce our carbon footprint, and solve one of the most serious problems in American society—the lack of retirement savings, especially for younger generations of workers.

And, by the way, we can also solve a lot of other problems, like water consumption at power plants (which is the second largest consumer of water as a sector, behind agriculture), drilling or importing oil to turn into gasoline, improving health regimes by encouraging transportation alternatives like bicycling and walking, and many others.

We can do this! *We have to do this.*

A person can get pretty cynical and frustrated after forty years in one career. Especially in an industry like electricity, where change usually happens at a snail's pace, though often for very good reasons. Investment horizons are 20-50 years out. If you make a seriously bad decision on what you are going to build, you'll pay for that mistake for decades! Which is why utility executives are very careful and conservative decision makers.

But consider these analogous sectors where change occurred really fast. In a short ten years, something like 60 percent of the American population got regular access to the internet and the valuable resources it provides. It took only two decades to convert pretty much the entire nation from a landline-wired communication system to a wireless cellular system. These are infrastructure systems, too.

China *quadrupled* the size of its electricity infrastructure in less than two decades! Similar to what happened in China, the US electricity system expanded by 6-7 percent annually post WWII to the early 1970s. That means it more than doubled in thirty years! More recently, the US electricity industry managed to add over 200,000 MW of new natural gas-fired power plants to a grid dominated by coal and nuclear in six years!

Think about the armaments this nation pumped out for the WWII war effort. That required a national mobilization of the citizenry, and private enterprises working closely with the federal government. But it got done! That's because everyone sacrificed. Everyone.

So, when someone chuckles and says "yeah, right!" at the thought of converting the US electric system to mostly carbon-free renewables in twelve years, shake them out of their stupor. We've accomplished much tougher goals. The collective will, the political will, and a good incentive structure are all that stand in the way.

All of us need to feel *viscerally*, and act upon a sense of personal responsibility and accountability for our contributions to climate change—and share a sense of national pride as, together, we work to mitigate it.

## THE CARBON IRA

The premise of the Carbon IRA is simple:

*Reward individual actions that reduce a person's carbon footprint by converting the avoided carbon into funds deposited in a retirement account.*

That's it!

Figure 7. Convert avoided carbon into retirement funds.

The *promise* of the Carbon IRA is that it addresses two seemingly intractable societal problems simultaneously:

1.  Global climate change.
2.  Inadequate retirement savings.

That's it! My work is done here.
Ah, may the world be so simple…

As I mentioned in the introduction, I've been following global climate change as an electricity industry professional since 1988, when James Hansen delivered his testimony to Congress about the warming of the planet. Every policy framework, proposal, or market-based solution I've ever reviewed—and I've probably had to review all of them at one time—has at least one fatal flaw.

## FATAL FLAW:

They result in relatively short-term behavior modifications.

The best examples are when gasoline prices go up, people drive less (less carbon out of the tailpipe). When consumers are convinced prices will remain high for a while, they buy smaller, more energy-efficient vehicles. When prices go back down, they revert to their original behaviors: driving more and driving large, gas-guzzling vehicles.

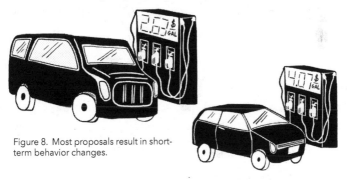

Figure 8. Most proposals result in short-term behavior changes.

Theoretically, consumer behaviors are induced in one of at least two ways: either through a regulatory mechanism (i.e., a law or policy) or "market forces." The reality is that markets are almost always influenced by regulatory mechanisms; the more mature the product or service, the more regulatory driven is the market. (For those of you who took Econ 101 and now believe you're an expert, or for any Ayn Rand accolytes out there, there is no such thing as pure market forces or an "invisible hand.")

Without pretending I am an economist, though, it is safe to say that energy prices are highly cyclical. When I purchased an SUV in 2001 when our family was growing, gasoline prices were around $2.00 gal. When I purchased a subcompact Honda Fit in 2008, gasoline prices were more like $4.00 and appeared to be rising indefinitely.

Now gas prices are low, they've been relatively low for many years,  and virtually all forecasts anticipate they will remain relatively low (barring repercussions from new war in the Middle East). Many people will see this as an opportunity to get a larger vehicle and drive more. The challenge in carbon economics is to overcome these fluctuating prices and behaviors.

Another good example of a temporary behavior change is a carbon tax. Many politicians and environmental advocates have attempted to address climate change by proposing a tax on carbon-emitting energy sources and redistributing the money to consumers (also a way to stimulate the economy).

This is also short-term stimulus, and short-sighted. It merely penalizes energy company suppliers who will eventually raise prices to recoup the loss. Once the temporary jolt to the economy is felt, consumers will in all likelihood return to former habits.

It is often said that companies don't pay taxes; consumers do, in the form of higher prices.

The Carbon IRA concept breaks this impasse. It offers a lifetime reward for a lifetime of a carbon-reducing behavior. If you commute by mass transit, carpool, or ride a bicycle to and from work, you should be rewarded over the period of that behavior. If you buy and use an electric vehicle in a region served largely by carbon-free electricity, you should be rewarded over the tens of thousands of miles you drive in that car.

There are other important benefits of a Carbon IRA:

1. It represents "new money," i.e., it's not money diverted from your paycheck so it doesn't sacrifice immediate economic output. When consumers save, it penalizes the economy short term because the money isn't put to work immediately.

2.  It's not a tax or a subsidy. Those who abhor new taxes or see subsidies as economic dislocations should favor an approach based solely on consumer choice.

3.  Since it is not a tax or subsidy, it doesn't require a government program. In fact, as I explain later, the best early adopters of Carbon IRA are profitable companies who can easily include a Carbon IRA option in their employee compensation programs.

4.  Companies routinely offer 401Ks and match savings and pension options, usually with automatic payroll deductions. Adding a Carbon IRA would not be that challenging.

5.  Those most likely to choose a Carbon IRA option will be young people who (1) have been "schooled" in climate change and don't require any convincing that the planet they live on may not be inhabitable by their offspring's offspring, (2) often leave college heavily in debt and can't find money for a mortgage, much less retirement savings, (3) have youth and vitality on their side, and can walk or bike to work, and (4) often champion other lifestyle choices, like vegetarian or veganism, which are significant carbon-avoiding practices.

Figure 9. Carbon IRA can be added to a menu of employee benefits.

For these reasons, and because it relies on consumer choice, the Carbon IRA should be non-partisan or bi-partisan politically. Of course, the government, which presumably needs to address climate issues, should get involved and support a Carbon IRA framework. My point is, though, it doesn't have to, especially not in the beginning.

## FOUR BROAD STEPS

Conceptually, the four steps to implement Carbon IRA are:

1. **Assign Carbon Value**. Each increment of avoided carbon has to be converted into a monetary value. This can be done by creating standards, using a market price for carbon, or otherwise assigning the value to the avoided carbon based on the funder's perceived urgency of the climate change crisis.

2. **Monitor and Track**. A sanctioned authority, government agency, or company has to track the avoided carbon from the continuous behavior, with appropriate validation and verification. I would propose, at least as a start, a voluntary system similar to tax filing, with the threat and penalties of a potential audit.

3. **Qualify Behaviors and Consumer Choices**. A sanctioned authority has to decide which behaviors qualify for the funds. Should taking the subway in Manhattan qualify, when the option of driving a passenger vehicle isn't really an option? What about the carbon avoided by eating vegan and displacing meat from factory farms? The calculations for some of these can be kind of ambiguous but it would depend on how aggressively the "authority" wishes to implement the program.

4. **Manage the Funds**. Once the behavior has taken place and been verified, and the avoided carbon has been monetized (converted into money), the funds have to be deposited into an account and managed by a recognized financial firm. This is in many ways the easiest part of the framework to visualize. Many companies manage savings, investment, and retirement accounts for their patrons.

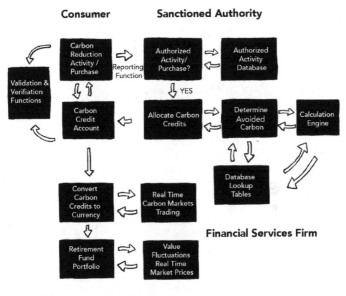

Figure 10. Carbon IRA flow diagram

Of course, there are many smaller decisions which have to be worked out for a successful program. For example, will the account be subject to fluctuations in the value of carbon in the carbon markets, just like stocks and bonds? Again, people make these kinds of decisions all the time. Nothing new here. But to start out, it's probably best that a fixed price for carbon be used and that the funds accrue interest just like a contribution from your paycheck.

## EARLY ADOPTERS

Any company, governmental organization, non-profit, etc., can implement a Carbon IRA. But some companies are better suited to be early adopters than others. Three categories of excellent candidates are the digital technology firms, electric utilities, and financial technology (fintech) firms.

Of these, the digital companies are probably best. Think companies like Microsoft, Amazon, Facebook, Apple, and Google. They already have aggressive programs to drive their firms and customers towards renewable energy, implement sustainable practices, have employees who skew towards younger age profiles, are highly profitable, have high stock valuations which allow them to pursue long-term business strategies and invest for the future (rather than pay profits out in stock dividends), and the technologies necessary to implement Carbon IRA are already in their portfolio!

In fact, I did a deep dive analysis into one of these company's internal programs and policies and discovered that a Carbon IRA offering to their tens of thousands of employees would only be a modest extension of their existing compensation programs, corporate strategies, and internal employee development programs.

This big five digital firm already has myriad internal "social responsibility" policies and procedures intended to drive their own company and their customers towards a low carbon future. The most impactful of these policies is that each internal business unit is charged a "carbon fee" for the carbon discharge impact of a project. In other words, when a business leader in this firm wants funding for a project, the accounting must include a fee charged for the carbon footprint. This is an added cost burden, additional inches on the height of the investment hurdle that the calculated internal rate of return of that project has to clear.

The funds from the internal carbon fees are then collected and directed to corporate energy efficiency, community sustainability, and renewable energy projects. In other words, money from carbon-producing aspects of the company's operations are diverted to invest in carbon-avoiding activities.

This same member of the "big five digital" peer group also has employee reward programs for suggesting and implementing actions which can be leveraged collectively to reduce the company's overall carbon footprint—including recycling, energy efficiency, and others.

So why not expand these policies and programs to include a Carbon IRA? How much more difficult would it be for such a company (they are coders and programmers, after all) to develop an app which monitors and tracks employees bicycling miles, for those who commute by bike? Or upload the data from a fitness tracker which shows the number of miles walked and the time of day, validating that the walking was done for commuting? Or, for carpoolers, to punch the equivalent of a clock or take a digital photo at the reserved premium parking space when they show up to work in a carpool?

These are not complicated tasks.

Electric utilities would also be natural early adopters of Carbon IRA. They could easily implement for their employees and, with the approval of their state public utility commissions, could invest in such programs for their ratepayers. In fact, Carbon IRA would create strong incentives for rapid displacement of fossil fuel-based electricity with renewable energy (solar, hydro, wind).

By encouraging their ratepayers to either install rooftop PV or buy electricity from renewable sources (green purchasing programs), utilities could create a strong feedback loop: Customers buy into long-term contracts for renewable energy, which supports the investment necessary to displace coal and gas-fired power plants with solar and wind.

Utilities are infrastructure companies, which means they have to plan and invest on a multi-decade basis.

Imagine if their customers have committed to renewable electricity purchases on a multi-year basis, incentivized by the retirement fund contributions. Ratepayer purchases and utility planning are now aligned for the long haul!

Utilities are also used as tax collectors for governments, too. After all, utilities are quasi-private firms; they earn a rate of return on invested assets that is set by a governmental authority, usually the public utility commission. So it doesn't seem like a great leap for them to also be agencies that collect retirement funds from carbon avoided by their ratepayers.

And the monthly utility bill, already a menu of costs, fees, taxes, etc., could serve as a mechanism for tracking avoided carbon, validating it (the utility *by design* monitors electricity consumption and could easily, by extension, monitor avoided carbon), and reporting it to the entity responsible for managing the retirement account.

In fact, every company that wants to promote the use of low- or no-carbon consumer choices would be well-served by implementing Carbon IRA both for employees and customers. For instance, companies that sell "smart" thermostats can add features that monitor and track avoided carbon and report those figures to the responsible authority. Automotive companies can incentivize the transition to electric vehicles, just like utilities can incentivize the transition to renewable power generation. And any company seeking to attract and retain savvy young workers can add Carbon IRA to its benefits package as an incentive.

One company in a class all by itself with respect to the feasibility of early Carbon IRA adoption sells both electric vehicles and solar PV systems. For reasons I elaborate on in Part II of this book, this company already has business units pursuing the major aspects of the YouTility vision. Imagine how such a firm would benefit by championing the Carbon IRA framework to drive EV and PV sales.

## WITH THE STROKE OF A PEN

Ultimately, the broad success of Carbon IRA will likely rest with government policies. I say this not because I wish to see another regulatory framework imposed on the electricity industry (or on the rest of us), but because the reality of the electricity industry is that it is regulatory-driven, whether directly (environmental laws, regulated rates of return on invested capital) or indirectly (need to meet strict customer delivery reliability criteria and ensure electricity is always available).

It would be great if Congress or a progressive state like California passed legislation supporting a Carbon IRA framework. And they probably would if someone sat in DC or Sacramento and doled out millions in lobbying funds to get the message out.

In the meantime, a more logical and fruitful approach might be to work with the Smart Cities movement. To me, Smart Cities sounds like the same vague, slide-deck driven set of ideas that brought us "smart grid" and "smart meters." The organizing principle of Smart Cities, however, is instructive: to integrate low carbon energy, digital and wireless technologies, mass transportation, city lighting, and other aspects of urban living into a common framework.

Now imagine if the top-down approach of a Smart City was combined with the bottom-up approach of Carbon IRA driving demand for Smart City features and design? That's a winning combination limited only by the imagination.

## CASE STUDY IDEAS

Speaking of imagination, it's always refreshing to see how people's brains begin to churn when they start thinking through the Carbon IRA framework. In this section, I present a compendium of some of the great ideas which have fallen out of such discussions.

I spoke with the CEO of a small financial technology firm (50 employees) which manages retirement accounts for its clients using strictly web-based automation tools. His words were to this effect: Our sweet spot is innovative ways to manage retirement accounts, so why couldn't we add a Carbon IRA option and offer it to our customers? He expressed an interest in implementing a pilot program within his company as a way to learn how to build the tools and processes. Unfortunately, at the present time, he is consumed with planning a strategic exit for the company.

A manager at a cooperative utility had the brilliant idea of offering Carbon IRA to his ratepayers, and raising the funds to seed the accounts through a small fee on electricity sold through electric vehicle charging stations owned and operated by the utility. Cooperative utilities are owned by its members (unlike investor-owned utilities which are "owned" by stockholders). Thus, they are ratepayers and owners at the same time. I love the idea of raising the funds through EV chargers because that also expands the utility's customer demand.

An interesting challenge he brought up is that his young employees want to live downtown and commute to the utility's suburban location. More and more, they want EVs. If this utility, the executive reasoned, put charging stations at their office location, it would not sacrifice revenue to the competing utility which has the city in its service territory. In other words, employees charge where they work rather than where they live, and the cooperative makes the money, not the investor-owned utility serving the city.

With a modest fee on EV charging, money is raised to reward the employees on the Carbon IRA program. This is win win win—the cooperative wins by increasing revenue generation, the employees win who want to drive EVs and participate in Carbon IRA, and the climate wins because gasoline-powered transportation miles are avoided.

The executive also noted that the utility had recently begun administering a program of giving credits in the corporate wellness program to employees who achieve "10,000 steps" of activity as monitored through a Fitbit or equivalent device. Rewarding credits for avoiding carbon isn't much different.

## Colleges and Universities

Institutes of higher education are business ecosystems unto themselves in many ways. Most are struggling to be responsive to rising costs, reduced state and federal funding, spiraling student debt, and are often hotbeds of academic and political activity around climate change. A few universities are in the vanguard of using carbon pricing internally in their business accounting.

Why not adapt Carbon IRA so that students can achieve some debt forgiveness by practicing behaviors which reduce their carbon footprint? This could also condition students during their college years for a lifetime of such behavior changes. One student noted that it would be pretty easy for the school food program to monitor campus food purchases and begin aggregating avoided carbon, such as through vegetarian or vegan eating.

Some universities gouge students on things like parking violations. Instead of being adversarial, why not discourage any use of a private automobile and encourage behaviors which improve health (walking, bicycling) and help the university "put their practices where their mouths are" when it comes to climate change.

### Governments

Filing tax returns is a major pain in the ass. That's because we tend to see it as the government taking our money, rather than as our obligation for the services the government provides.

While the federal government (and some states) withhold taxes from paychecks, more and more taxpayers are "free agents" and pay their taxes quarterly.

Regardless, though, we "true up" before April 15 for the previous year by filling out forms and either getting a refund or sending in payment. Our analysis of our tax liability is based on complicated forms, but what numbers we insert on each line is largely up to us. In other words, it's mostly a voluntary system, with the threat of an audit as a compliance "stick."

The tax free retirement account contribution can swing the refund or payment by a wide margin. I make a contribution to my IRA every year. My retirement funds manager records it. But to my knowledge, the IRS never actually verifies if I have actually put that money in an account.

It's a voluntary system.

It would be straightforward for the federal or state government to add a form called the "carbon avoidance" form. Taxpayers would aggregate all of their carbon-avoiding activities, and delineate them on the form. I put in miles that I use my car for business. Why couldn't I put in miles that I biked instead of took a car? Smart taxpayers would ensure that they had means to verify these behaviors should the IRS come a calling. Each year, the government entity can assign the value of carbon for that year, or make it fixed. The monetized avoided carbon would then have to be deposited in a retirement account, just like your IRA or 401K contribution.

## It's All in the Details

For an actual situation, the details would have to be worked out and tweaked as experience is gained and lessons learned, just like all systems and processes. I'm simply illuminating that we're not really stretching very far from real-life situations we deal with all the time, whether at the consumer level or the organizational level.

Carbon isn't that much different from dollars. In fact, the sooner we begin to equate the two in our minds, thereby understanding the value of avoiding, or at least lessening, planetary damage, the faster we'll make the transition to non- or low-carbon lifestyles.

## CHALLENGES

Of course, implementing the Carbon IRA framework does pose challenges, but they can be addressed.

For instance, determining the baseline behavior is a challenge. Let's say I want to monetize the avoided carbon for keeping my thermostat at 82°F in the summer. What is my baseline behavior to which that will be compared? Would the authority use the average temperature setting for all of America, the region in which I live, or the average of my last several years of usage?

How do you differentiate between an EV driven in a region with 80 percent renewable electricity in the grid and one with 40 percent? Do you compare the avoided carbon to the average vehicle in America, or to the previous car this person drove?

A utility, for example, could determine from having data from thousands of smart thermostats that the average ratepayer setting is 76°F in its service territory. It could design a sliding scale of carbon value for customers willing to keep the thermostat between 77-82°F.

Predictability is also critical for utilities to avoid paying for expensive peaking generation, the electricity units which have to be turned on during the hottest or coldest hours of the day. Ratepayers should be rewarded not only for avoiding the carbon to maintain a higher temperature but for helping to make the utility's demand more predictable.

Today, many utilities have programs which will reward you with money for such behaviors. It wouldn't be a stretch to convert those programs so that they reward with funds deposited into the retirement account, or funds reimbursed which the ratepayer is obligated to deposit in the retirement account.

Similar issues would have to be reasoned out for the EV example. Ratepayers who charge their EVs at night (when electricity is less expensive) should also be rewarded for avoiding the carbon associated with that electricity. A utility could simply decide that if their electricity generating mix is 50% renewable and 50% fossil, then EV charging carbon credits can be apportioned respectively.

There are many issues like these but they can be thought through and resolved. We're able to send robots to Mars to take photos and spacecraft to asteroids to collect soil samples. We listen for voices from outer space. We inserted the Affordable Care Act into the massive health care insurance business and added credits and lines to report about them on IRS tax forms. We can tackle difficult ideas.

Perhaps the most important question an early adopter has to answer is, "What is a fair price for avoided carbon?" One knee-jerk answer is to simply adopt the market price. There are carbon trading markets, just like there are debt, equities (stocks), currencies, and commodities trading mechanisms. Over the last ten years, the price of carbon in these markets has ranged from $5-200 per ton.

Back-of-envelope calculations will quickly show that it takes quite an effort for a consumer to "avoid" a ton of carbon output. If that carbon is priced at the low end of this range, just for argument's sake, it's not going to result in much of an incentive.

At the high end of this range, though, the contribution is far from negligible. And when several behaviors are combined and compounded over the years, the contributions really can lead to a much more affluent retirement!

Over time, though, one could forecast that the value of carbon will escalate as the climate change impacts become more acute. And a company adopting a Carbon IRA program could artificially inflate the carbon-to-dollar conversion rate to "prime the pump," so to speak, AND make the program attractive to the early participants.

In fact, maybe the better question is not what the fair price of carbon is, *but what is the price commensurate with the threat of irreversible climate change in twelve years* and the threat of penniless retirees decade to decade? The fact is, organizations attempt to quantify difficult qualitative parameters all the time.

The victims in airline disasters, terrorist events (e.g., 9/11), and other calamities are "valued" in compensation proceedings for families or heirs. Participants in class-action lawsuits sue for damages which have to be estimated. Insurance companies pay out for damages, injury, and death based on fuzzy estimates of value. Reparations to victims of political and societal prejudice and racism have to be calculated based on nebulous value concepts.

So while the "market" value of a ton of avoided carbon isn't much of an incentive, the *threat value* based on twelve years to get our collective act in gear could be one or two orders of magnitude larger. Under the Obama administration, the "social cost" of carbon was calculated to be over $40/ton; the Trump administration changed the methodology so that it came out to under $10/ton.

We haven't even begun to value the benefit of millions of future retirees less dependent on social security, or the value in the health and medical system of people who are exercising more, eating better, etc.

Another challenge, as many have pointed out in my presentations, is that the reason why the retirement savings rate is so anemic is that people have difficulty focusing on what's good for them in fifty years, rather than what they desire today. But this isn't a challenge specific to Carbon IRA; it's a challenge with savings (and human beings) generally.

This is why social security is based on a small percentage extracted from employee paychecks every pay period, and why employers offer pension programs also supported by the government. It's also why employers deduct an amount from your paycheck for a supplemental savings program, and often will match that contribution.

The truth is, most people have to be forced to save.

One premise of Carbon IRA is that when a person, especially a young adult who needs no convincing of the gravity of climate change, is saving for his or her retirement and "saving the planet" in their own small way, that person will be doubly responsible about socking away money.

As I show later in the "historical context" section, the IRA originally was conceived and proposed to overcome the general tendency not to save. So was the pension. So was the 401K, and the company match programs.

Yes, retirement saving does, for all intents and purposes, have to be imposed on most people. But this argues *for* including a Carbon IRA option in the compensation package menu of options rather than against the concept.

The final broad challenge is validating that the behaviors are, in fact, taking place to track the avoided carbon. How does the "authority" confirm that a commuter biked to work five days last week, or took the bus, or drove an electric vehicle instead of a gasoline-powered one?

Figure 11. What authority verifies the amount of carbon avoided?

Electric vehicles are equipped with powerful computers and the miles and time of day can easily be tracked, totaled, and uploaded to a central data repository or reported to the vehicle owner to insert on a company or government form. Those who own and drive EVs say that every bit of data about their car is uploaded to a central server.

I use an app on my phone that tracks the miles I ride on my bike. My wife uses one when she walks or bikes to work. We could agree to have that data reported to the responsible agency with time stamps.

In short, there are apps for all these challenges, and they're already used in other applications like health and activity tracking, investing, insurance, banking, utility usage, etc. They just need to be adapted for the specific purposes of implementing Carbon IRA.

Yes, unethical people can hack into the apps. To those who argue that people will cheat and game the system, well, no framework has solved the fundamental vagaries of the human condition. I mean, federal and state governments base taxation largely on voluntary compliance, with the threat of an audit and backed up by such required reporting of income by employers as payroll deductions and 1099 and K-1 reporting for freelancers or partners in limited liability companies—most of it transmitted to the IRS electronically. There's no reason to believe that violations and non-compliance for a Carbon IRA program will be any worse than paying taxes.

And yes, there are digital security and privacy issues as well. Let's face it, your phone and your social media apps probably know more about you than you do, unless you've been diligent about maintaining your privacy and security. Even then, those apps and platforms still record all this stuff, they are just limited by what they can do with it.

As we discover every time there is a mass shooting or a disaster somewhere, we are also constantly under surveillance by security cameras. Just when I was getting used to self-checkout at most of the stores I frequent, I learned that some of them photograph you every time you use the system! Let's be honest. Is carbon avoidance monitoring, tracking, aggregating, monetizing, and depositing into accounts any less secure and "public" than online and wireless banking? Once you begin to think of carbon like money, most of these challenges become surmountable in a hurry.

And those whose political opinions have been recorded on Facebook for eternity shouldn't be too concerned about all of their carbon-avoidance behaviors and purchases being recorded for posterity. In the latter case, at least you are being rewarded with retirement money and doing your part to beat back that 12-year doomsday clock.

The challenge, really, is to knit together the various participants and apps so that a comprehensive and easy-to-use framework can be offered to participants.

## HISTORICAL CONTEXT

Retirement accounts have long been used as instruments of behavior modification. Small businesses, large corporations, and institutions offer pensions and contributions to supplementary retirement savings accounts for good reasons.

Historically, the practice arose from a legacy of labor relations and government demands that companies share more of their profits with workers. More recently, competition for talent drives compensation programs. Finding, training, and retaining human talent has always been one of the prime challenges of running a company. Pensions and retirement benefits keep employees from leaving. When a company invests in an employee, the employee invests in the company.

Governments understand the value of private pensions and retirement savings, too. That's why such contributions are "tax-advantaged." And if private firms pay for their employees' old age as a reward for many years, or a life-time, of employment, that means the government doesn't have to dole out that money. The more a citizen takes care of himself or herself, aided by the private sector, the less of a burden that person will be on the government.

As a recent article in the *New York Times* reminded, the 401K savings concept isn't even forty years old. The term 401k refers to a section of the tax code that allows a taxpayer to defer paying taxes on money set aside for retirement.

Apparently, it originated in 1980 when a consultant created a savings plan based on this tax advantage for a client, but the client rejected it as too risky. So, the consultant tried it at his own firm. Today, the 401k is the most common employee-sponsored retirement plan.

The individual retirement account (IRA) was developed by the federal government around the same time. Taxpayers can make an annual contribution to the IRA account and that amount is deducted from the total income subject to federal tax that year. Roth IRAs are a way to pay the taxes in the year the contribution is made, rather than paying the taxes in the year of retirement as the money is withdrawn.

Really, the only difference with a Carbon IRA is that carbon is treated like money. That's why carbon trading markets were developed and are run by the same financial management firms that run other markets in commodities, securities, and currencies. If we begin to treat carbon as if it has monetary value, people will adapt their behaviors and consumer habits as if discharging carbon dioxide is tantamount to wasting money (and not just harming the environment)!

## ANEMIC RETIREMENT ACCOUNTS

Every study about retirement savings rates of Americans reveals dismal and disturbing results. The vast majority of Americans do not save enough for retirement. Even as they live longer and longer. In fact, our "retirement" years may soon be as long as our "working" years. Although estimates may differ, that conclusion is a common thread.

One study showed that the average American with a retirement account between the ages of 55-64 has saved $85,000. The average American adult between 21 and retirement age has far less than this. That's because, according to a *New York Times* article (Oct 19, 2017), one-third of all Americans have saved nothing for retirement (although many of the persons in this "average" are probably young and not yet that worried about retirement).

Another *New York Times* article (March 3, 2017) noted that close to 40 million Americans work for an employer without a payroll deduction program for retirement.

And here's yet another statistic: 45 percent of all American households have no retirement account. The Government Accountability Office (GAO) reported in a 2017 study that the average American between 55 and 64 had saved only $107,000 for retirement!

The Economic Policy Institute (EPI) showed slightly more encouraging data in a 2013 study (using data from the Federal Reserve Board's Survey of Consumer Finances) but not by much. The mean amount of retirement wealth for all families was $96,000. Adults aged 32-37 had between $30,000 and $35,000 saved while adults between 56-61 had around $164,000 in retirement wealth.

How much you should save of course depends on many factors—how long you expect to live, how much money you plan to spend in retirement, etc.

But nobody who studies and reports on this stuff is arguing that the vast majority of Americans are even close to saving what they will need to supplement social security and their pension, without taking a big hit to their current lifestyles.

As a reminder, IRAs, 401Ks, and Roth accounts are tax-advantaged. IRAs, for example, allow you to put money aside, and reduce your income burden subject to federal tax that year. The percentage of your annual income that can be set aside has changed over the years, but is usually between 5-10 percent of income.

That's a sizable tax break, similar to the mortgage deduction, suggesting how important both are (though for a different reasons) to the economic health of the nation. Another tax advantage is that, while the income stream is taxed after you retire and receive disbursements, that tax rate will generally be much lower than your tax bracket while you are in your prime earning years.

The Obama administration started a new program called the MyRA predicated on investing in government bonds, but it has since been discontinued.

Think about young adults working for less than ten years. Many have significant college debt burdens to pay off, and many of them, as they head into their 30s, will get married and have families and undertake home mortgages and other kinds of debt (if they can afford to and still manage their college debt). Their ability to set aside retirement funds is and will remain severely restrained.

And in case you haven't looked recently, social security benefits aren't exactly escalating. Your benefits are capped after you've paid into the program for a certain amount of time. As a matter of fact, the government has been threatening to reduce retirement benefits almost as long as I've been in the workforce—and that means reductions have been threatened for four decades! One of these days, the government may succeed and make good on its threats.

Now is an excellent time to push for a Carbon IRA. The US House of Representatives recently passed a bipartisan bill addressing savings and retirement. One of the provisions allows workers to contribute to an IRA indefinitely, rather than up to the age of 70 ½, according to a June 4, 2019 article in *The New York Times*.

This would mean you could continue getting rewarded for your carbon avoiding behaviors while you are retired! The larger point is that the government is addressing these issues and wouldn't some real innovation be welcome?

## VULNERABLE YOUNG ADULTS

The college debt crisis continues to percolate under the American economy like the magma of an imminent volcano. Forgiving all or much of this debt has become a plank in the progressive political agenda.

Even Betsy DeVos, President Trump's Secretary of Education and self-styled champion of any type of school that isn't a public school, has admitted that this is a crisis jeopardizing the country's future.

Several years ago, friends of mine—she got an MFA in her 30s and her spouse got a PhD in his late 30s—told me they'd be paying their college loans well into retirement! Someone else we know, a registered nurse who is also a doctor of chiropractic, has such a high student loan debt that when she and her husband went to buy a house, she couldn't put her name on the loan papers even though her annual income is significantly higher than his.

Two thirds of all college students incur some level of debt, and college debt is the second highest debt category with only mortgages being higher. It is even higher than credit card debt, the one economists always worry about when recessions loom. The debt load depends on the type of school, public or private, and loan term, and you can find your own numbers to illustrate how deep this crisis is, but the one that hits home for me is that the average student owes between $25,000 - $40,000 upon receiving their college diploma! And today, according to one source, two

Figure 13. College debt load is not only unsustainable, it is a drain on the economy

thirds of the total borrowing is for loans to pay off the earlier loans! That is simply unsustainable.

It doesn't take a genius to gauge the negative impact on the general economy. If a young adult is paying $200-400 monthly for college loans, that money isn't going to pay for healthcare, autos, houses, furniture, mortgages, starting a family, or investing in some type of entrepreneurial activity. And facing such a high debt burden makes setting aside money for retirement each month that much more difficult.

The conclusion one has to draw here is that Americans of all ages don't save enough for retirement, but young Americans are far less able to, even if they wanted to. All this, by the way, is happening in the ten years after the "Great Recession," the worst economic crisis since the Great Depression, and at a time during which real wage growth has been stagnant. And those who entered the work force during the Great Recession were hit with the triple whammy of hard-to-find jobs, college debt, and wage stagnation.

One variation of the Carbon IRA could be to put the monetized avoided carbon to work paying down student debt. However, this would be more complicated because the banks which lent the money have to be "made whole" and the only way that could be done is if the federal government shoves the money their way and takes the debt on its own balance sheet (much like the way the banks were rescued after the 2007-2008 crash).

## YOUNG ADULTS AT THE NEXUS

Young adults, notwithstanding the miseries they face with college debt, inadequate pay in employment, etc. are, happily, those most likely to understand climate change and see it as an existential threat.

Veterans returning from WWII had a different understanding of the world as a result of their experiences. They propelled the American economic miracle that lasted until the early 1970s (and that was, arguably, enabled by higher tax rates on top earners and a generous G.I. Bill that sent a generation of young men to college largely debt free).

The post-war world was built upon a consumption-based economy and adults during this period were hell bent on consuming! Today's young adults understand that over-consumption is what has led us to the climate change crisis and the ticking 12-year clock. They have a different understanding of the world because of what they've been taught in school, and what they are experiencing in terms of climate change, extreme weather events, economic malaise, etc.

And while getting a lot of flak in some media outlets for caring more about their avocado toast and expensive cappuccinos, they could be the next "greatest generation," representing those willing to break the consumption principle as an economic good and replace it with an ethos of conservation as economic good—as long as there is a commensurate reward structure.

Americans were willing to make sacrifices during WWII. Soldiers, sailors, airmen, marines and nearly 60,000 nurses gave up their livelihoods and many gave their lives. Privately-owned factories retooled their assembly lines for armaments production, and citizens back home recycled and scrimped and saved and bought war bonds to support the "war effort." The American "community" understood it was fighting a great evil and that we had to collectively stand with our allies to combat tyranny. Everyone—from school children collecting scrap metal to those fighting on the front—had a role to play.

Today, we are facing a similar existential crisis in global climate change, and the Carbon IRA framework can re-inject this ethos of sacrifice for the greater good in collective American behavior. It is up to us to rise to the challenge.

## BACK OF ENVELOPE CALCULATIONS

Before we review a few examples of how a Carbon IRA would build savings, let me first stipulate that the program can only be a supplement to existing retirement set-asides. Even if you live and work from a cave, you won't be spending your retirement cruising around the world on luxury liners with your Carbon IRA savings.

A market-leaning economist would tell you that the only legitimate way to "value" carbon for the purposes of savings is through a carbon trading market. And that's the crux of the challenge—the price of carbon in the carbon markets is ridiculously low and certainly does not reflect the magnitude of the global climate crisis or the critical nature of the 12-year countdown-to-catastrophe clock.

In recent years, the price of carbon in the markets has been between \$5-12/ton (of $CO_2$ equivalent). The highest I've seen the carbon price in the markets over the last fifteen years is \$300/ton. That's quite a difference.

Why does the value fluctuate so wildly in the markets? The simplest explanation is that the price follows how seriously governments threaten to institute carbon reducing policies. The high values were associated with the period when the US House of Representatives had passed a carbon "cap and trade" bill which would have allowed carbon monetizing and trading as if it were like any other security, debt instrument, commodity, or currency.

By imposing a cap on overall carbon emissions across the nation, the value of each avoided ton escalated. This represents another fundamental of economics: scarcity pricing. Gold and diamonds have high value because they are rare. Other goods have high prices because their availability may be naturally or artificially constrained.

For the last few years, carbon prices in the markets have been very low, because there is no overall cap (no scarcity) and policies to lower carbon have been perceived by the market as unrealistic, or not an immediate threat. Also, many carbon reducing actions are now proceeding on fundamental economics, e.g., the cost of generating a kilowatt of electricity (not a kilowatt hour continuously through out the day and night) with solar or wind is lower in many regions of the country than the cost of burning fossil fuels.

Is the price of avoided carbon commensurate with the 12-year ticking time clock?

The examples below will show that, even at $500/ton, the highest value I've seen in projections of carbon value into the future, the retirement savings over a lifetime of work is modest at best. But the good news is that the savings is not insignificant! The sums can truly enhance a retirement savings portfolio.

Here's one of the best examples for Carbon IRA. A friend of mine in Tucson commuted by bicycle to his job for ten years. It was rare if he commuted by other means. The round trip was 30 miles. To keep the math easy, I calculated that he biked 7,500 miles annually, or 75,000 vehicle-miles avoided over the ten year period. Using just the gross average discharge of 1 lb $CO_2$ exhausted from a car per mile, this commuter avoided 37.5 tons of $CO_2$.

Figure 14. Bike to work and earn money for your retirement

At \$10/ton, a decade of pedaling to work nets this bicycle enthusiast a whopping \$375 in his Carbon IRA. However, at a projected value of \$300/ton, his Carbon IRA funds would be \$11,250. Now, if this commuter bicycled over a 40-year career, he's close to \$50,000!

So if the price of carbon more realistically reflected the looming calamity of climate change, actions such as bicycling to work could result in meaningful retirement savings.

You are probably thinking, well, anyone can pick arbitrary values and make something look good. That's true. In fact, I wrote a book about that, *Painting By Numbers: How to Sharpen Your BS Detector and Smoke Out the Experts.*

But guess what? People in positions of power and influence do this all the time! For example, the EPA under the Obama administration used a value of around $50/ton in calculating the "social cost of carbon;" when the Trump administration came in, officials changed the methodology so that the social cost of carbon would be between $1-7/ton.

That's a huge difference. Of course, it reflects the *politics* of carbon more than the science or economics of climate change. The price of carbon selected for a Carbon IRA program could reflect the ethical values of the company more than the value of carbon in the commodity market.

A company serious about "social responsibility" and sustainability should, in other words, select a value of carbon for a Carbon IRA program that reflects its own assessment of the gravity of climate change, not what traders looking to make a buck think it is worth in the "market."

Here's another way to "goose" the benefits of the program. Rather than assume the car this bicyclist wasn't using is an "average" car with respect to carbon out the tailpipe, use more realistic specs from the year/make/model the cyclist actually owned. If he's riding to work to avoid driving an old, inefficient model, it could double the rate of carbon displaced, thereby quickly doubling the benefit!

Another favorite example of mine is the avoided carbon of the vegan lifestyle. My two daughters are vegan/vegetarian. I like this example because I get to be juvenile and use the words farts and belches.

Cows—specifically cow belches and, to a lesser degree, cow farts—are a major contributor to carbon footprint and climate change. The gas is largely methane which is twenty times as bad as $CO_2$ as a warming agent in the atmosphere. Estimates of the carbon intensity of diets ranging from meat lover to vegan show that the vegan diet could be less than half the carbon intensity of a meat lovers, or 1.5 tons $CO_2e$ (equivalent) per person compared to 3.3 tons $CO_2e$.

Figure 15. Even cows contribute to climate change

Avoiding 1.8 tons $CO_2$ annually would convert to $540 a year socked away in the Carbon IRA. Over forty years, that would grow to $21,600. That's real money, too!

Now, it might be a little more difficult to validate what a person eats three times a day over forty years. I suppose an "authority" could request or demand grocery receipts to show the typical composition of the daily meals.

Although it's a little spooky to realize this, grocery stores retain records of your food purchases and sell that data (in generic form, supposedly) to marketers and use it to determine what to stock, inventory control, etc.

A Carbon IRA participant could agree to have that data uploaded to the responsible authority. For many, perhaps this is an acceptable invasion of privacy for a growing retirement account? Or, they could do it the old-fashioned way—collect receipts and have them on hand should the Carbon IRA police demand an audit.

Let's now look at two examples which, frankly, will make a lot more sense for most people.

My household consumed 1800 kWh of electricity in one month two years ago, or taking that average over the year, 21,600 kWh. Over 30 years, that would be 650,000 kWh. As you'll see in the YouTility section of this book, it's not a stretch to assume that close to all of this electricity use could be displaced by rooftop solar PV and storage, at least in my part of the country.

For the purposes of this example, let's assume that the home is off-grid. A rough figure for back-of-the-envelope (BOE) calculations is that 1 kWh results in 1 lb $CO_2e$. So the avoided carbon here is approximately 300 tons. If we monetize that at the rate we've been using, \$300/ton $CO_2e$, that's \$90,000.

Not only is this more than chump change, this is larger than the retirement savings of the average American close to retirement! And we haven't even started accounting for interest on the funds over time. We'll get to that.

Finally, let's evaluate an EV over a gasoline-powered one. The average American puts around 12,000 miles on his/her car every year. That's 480,000 miles over four decades, a typical working life. To keep the math easy, let's round that up to 500,000 miles.

Earlier, we used a BOE figure of 1 lb $CO_2e$ per mile. So that EV will avoid 500,000 lbs of $CO_2$, or 250 tons. Using our other BOE figure of \$300/ton of $CO_2e$, driving an EV instead of a gas-powered vehicle could net \$75,000 in the Carbon IRA. That figure also is comparable to the funds accrued by the average American nearing retirement.

## WE'RE TALKING REAL MONEY!

Back-of-the-envelope calculations are dangerous and can be misleading. But you can begin to see a larger picture here, can't you?

Let's say an aggressive Carbon IRA saver undertakes *all four* of these actions illustrated above—bicycling to work, eating vegan, rooftop solar PV and storage, and replacing a gasoline-powered car with an EV. Over a working life, the funds, before interest is accounted for, total $236,600. This, wonder of wonders, is a pretty healthy savings, relative to today's averages!

What does adding the interest on top of this do? Again, to keep the math simple, let's assume that $6,000 is deposited into the Carbon IRA each year. I went to a standard online compound interest calculator, plugged in 4.5 percent annually over 40 years, and the balance at the end of that period tops $700,000!

Now we're talking about a retirement account that can truly take care of someone, especially if it is supplemented by social security, Medicare, pension, etc.

Don't forget that I used a value for $CO_2e$ that is at the high end (for our purposes here, the optimistic end) of the forecasted range. $300/ton $CO_2e$ may not be realistic from a commodity price perspective. But if you used even half this amount, the calculations still net $350,000 over forty years. And given the 12-year ticking clock looming over us, a $300/ton $CO_2$e may in fact be commensurate with the magnitude and future costs of dealing with the fallout of unremediated global climate change.

I'm not pretending that a Carbon IRA should be one's sole lifeline into retirement. I am strongly suggesting, though, that the savings could be significant enough to supplement other retirement accounts.

And let's recall the principal moral authority of a Carbon IRA—to create a long-term incentive/reward for people to choose behaviors and consumer practices which lower carbon footprint.

Relative to the anemic retirement savings rates today, each of the behaviors illustrated results in significant sums individually! When they are combined, as Senator Proxmire famously said long ago, "pretty soon we're talking about real money."

## ANALOGIES ELSEWHERE

If any of this comes across as new regulatory burdens on citizens, nanny-state stuff, violations of our liberties, and all that, it shouldn't. Governments impose all manner of laws, subsidies, incentives, carrots, and sticks, to get us to "make good choices." So do corporations.

Auto insurance companies use in-vehicle cameras and data uploads to validate whether you are less of a risk as

Figure 16. Participation will have to be monitored

a driver than the average insured person, and then they give you a break on your premium if you prove it.

Home insurers give you a break if you have smoke detectors in the home and keep them in good working order. And have you ever filled out your health insurance forms and admitted that you are a "smoker?" Boy, will that make your premiums skyrocket! But today, health insurers encourage their customers to exercise, because fitness is correlated with better health.

Many large companies which offer health insurance to their employees also offer breaks on membership fees to fitness facilities or even have such facilities on their campuses. There also are programs associated with Medicare to get older Americans into exercise programs at clubs and fitness facilities. I recently learned of a firm that offers "vitality credits" to employees based on steps monitored with a FitBit. The credits are monetized and added to the employee's Health Savings Account

All of these are means to encourage people to make better choices rather than mandate that they do so.

## THE POLICY IMPERATIVE

The best evidence for at least considering a Carbon IRA framework is that little else in the policy arena appears to be working. And what is working can be accelerated by Carbon IRA (and YouTility).

To sum up and simplify what's happened over the last twenty years, the Bush administration was a big fan of RD&D programs and took climate science seriously, but they took business interests even more seriously.

Then the Obama administration appeared on the scene and pushed carbon policies aggressively. The Democratic Party controlled Congress during the first two years of the Obama administration and came close to passing a carbon cap and trade scheme, but couldn't close the deal. Eventually one version passed the House, but couldn't clear the Senate. Environmental groups have long been advocating for carbon taxes. But broad new taxing schemes are not popular with either political party.

Obama's was a policy crew that believed climate change was a real and significant threat. I know. I interacted with a few members of the committees on energy and environment for Obama's campaign. However, for the most part, Obama's goals evolved around phasing out coal and providing subsidies for renewables and EVs.

In fact, the Obama administration was successful in passing generous tax breaks for electric and hybrid vehicle purchases and for rooftop solar PV, and the majority of states have enacted some form of renewable portfolio standard which requires utilities to install more renewable energy systems, passing the costs through to the ratepayers. And they were able to spread around a significant amount of money through the American Reinvestment and Recovery Act (ARRA) to seed lower carbon footprint objectives, but much of this went to technology demonstration programs.

Frankly, like previous government programs of this type, much of the funds were extravagantly wasted on failed projects. Intentions were good. Results not so much. In hindsight, it was all too wrapped up in the financial crisis of 2007-2008. But ultimately, many technologies did make progress along the curve towards commercial viability.

Then Donald Trump, someone who claims climate change is a Chinese hoax, took office. His goal is to protect the coal industry and coal executives (and to shield and promote the oil and gas industry, as well). In fact, he's out to undo everything Obama did and that includes anything Obama did to protect the planet. But the larger point is that the federal government has muzzled scientists, and policy work and leadership on carbon reduction and climate change policy at the federal level has ground to a halt. In fact, as I write, the Trump Administration is attempting to fire many of the scientists in the Department of Agriculture working on climate change-related research.

And on the global stage, every few years responsible nations get together to work on and even agree to international treaties addressing carbon and climate change, but compliance is largely voluntary and much of what is accomplished is rich nations agreeing to subsidize poor nations, and poor nations demanding that they be allowed to become rich nations without onerous carbon constraints. And under the Trump Administration, the US's participation in such programs has largely been halted.

Overall, most policies implemented or proposed during the last twenty years fall into the following buckets:

1. Taxing the largest emitters of carbon—usually carbon dioxide and methane—and either adding the funds to the government's revenues or

distributing the funds to consumers as a way to "goose" the economy and accelerate spending,

2. Adding an "entry into the economic system" fee on carbon at its source (coal mines, oil/gas fields) and at ports of entry on carbon-bearing energy from abroad, mostly oil and natural gas,

3. Imposing environmental regulatory burdens on fossil fuels onerous enough to drive toward low- and non-carbon energy sources,

4. Instituting a carbon "cap and trade" market in which the overall carbon "cap" allowed is ratcheted down over time to increase value of avoided carbon,

5. Mandating carbon-free sources of electricity through minimum EV purchases or renewable portfolio standards (mandates that a certain percentage of electricity production come from renewables, primarily solar and wind),

6. One-time subsidies which incentivize the purchase of rooftop solar PV, energy efficient appliances, and electric vehicles,

7. Ratifying international agreements which drive countries towards lower carbon intensity and future targets for carbon emissions,

8. Increasing RD&D funds to cultivate new products and services which reduce carbon footprint, or

sequester or recycle the carbon discharged from industrial processes,

9.  Utility net metering under which customers buy or lease roof top solar panels and sell the electricity back to the utility at a much higher rate than the utility's wholesale costs.

Some variations of these policies and programs have been moving forward almost as long as my near-forty-year career in the electricity industry. While many of them have resulted in some progress towards reducing carbon intensity, over 90 percent of scientists working in related fields believe adverse carbon-induced climate impacts are accelerating, not diminishing.

For most of those four decades, I've kept my ear pretty close to the ground on global warming science and policies. When the Carbon IRA idea came to me, I did lots of research to determine if the idea was truly as unique as I thought. Turns out it is. I have found only vague minimal reference to creating a long-term reward structure for reducing an individual's carbon footprint.

For example, *Legal Pathways to Deep Decarbonization in the United States* (2018), while a great compendium of climate change policies and actions, does not include a long-term individual reward structure like Carbon IRA.

Even in *The Oxford Handbook of The Macroeconomics of Global Warming*, there is only one chapter/paper that comes remotely close, titled "Climate Change and Intergenerational Well-being," by celebrated economist Jeffrey D Sachs, then Director of the Earth Institute at Columbia University.

In his paper, Sachs argues for "intergenerational fiscal transfers (public debt) to allocate the burdens and benefits of climate change mitigation across generations without the need to trade off one generation's well-being for another's."

It's an important thesis because poor countries complain that while rich countries reap the benefits of a high-carbon intensity, consumer-based economy, developing countries are asked to pay a higher price today for less carbon tomorrow. In other words, I (today) bear the cost burden, you (in the future) reap the reward. In the meantime, you enjoy the luxuries of a carbon intensive lifestyle.

A similar objection is raised about the young generation versus the older generation in developed nations. Why should the economic output of the younger generation be penalized by carbon when the generation ahead of them enjoyed all the advantages of carbon-rich largesse?

Sachs's methodology addresses this gap. Nowhere, though, does he mention the use of retirement funds as a reward into the future for reducing carbon footprint today.

## THE CRISIS WE FACE

The latest Inter-governmental Panel on Climate Change (IPCC) report concludes that average global temperatures could rise by up to 2° Celsius as early as 2030. That's only a decade and change away! For anyone who has raised kids, you know how fast they grow from birth to becoming teenagers. A decade goes by very quickly.

If you read the summary of the report, it's clear that the "conversation" today among experts is not about avoiding global climate change or even returning climate patterns to pre-industrial levels, or even the climate patterns we older folks would recognize from our youth. No, it's

about how to limit the impacts of the predicted change to something between (a) wiping out humanity and (b) minimizing the severity of the impacts to the greatest number of people.

Figure 17. Glaciers are melting, sea levels are rising

In other words, the wound is deep and the blood is flowing and all we can do now is staunch the bleeding. Or, more appropriately, the glaciers are melting, and we can't stop the massive volumes of water from making sea levels rise to dangerous levels.

The 2019 Fourth National Climate Assessment, a report issued to Congress by the US Global Change Research Program (with the National Oceanic and Atmospheric Administration as the lead agency), is only the latest comprehensive summary of climate change and its impacts. But the threat level was elevated from previous reports.

The consequences are forecasted to be graver and sooner than experts thought just a few years ago.

The opening sentence in many ways says it all: "Earth's climate is now changing faster than at any point in the history of modern civilization, primarily as a result of human activities." Everyone should read the summary of the report, but here are the highlight bullets as a refresher:

- Annual average temperatures have increased by 1.8°F across the contiguous United States since the beginning of the 20th century.
- With substantial and sustained reductions in greenhouse gas emissions (e.g., consistent with the very low scenario), the increase in global annual

average temperature relative to preindustrial times could be limited to less than 3.6°F (2°C). Without significant greenhouse gas mitigation, the increase in global annual average temperature could reach 9°F or more by the end of this century.

Think about a future in which every day the temperature is a few degrees warmer than we experience now. Shifts like this—along with changing weather patterns—will create almost unimaginable changes to the ecosystem we share with all other living things.

Regardless of what some elected officials believe about climate change, these are the reasoned, dispassionate conclusions of the most respected global scientists and experts working in the field and are backed by decades of data collection, assessment, modeling, and number crunching. And while only between 50-60 percent of ordinary folks believe climate change is a serious threat, well over 90 percent of scientists studying climate are on board.

Let's be clear: What we're talking about now are desperate and immediate measures to limit the warming so that the average temperature rise is closer to the 3.6°F number and nowhere near the 9°F upper boundary. Essentially, what that means, according to the IPCC report, is that the net growth in carbon discharges to the atmosphere has to be reduced to zero by the middle of the century.

## CARBON, CARBON EVERYWHERE!

So how do we get to net zero carbon discharges when, according to the *Exxon Mobil World Energy Report of 2018*, world population is expected to increase from 7.4 billion to 9.2 billion by 2040? While one billion people today with no access to electricity yearn for the same modern conveniences, health benefits, and lifestyle luxuries electricity provides to the rest of us, how do we make electricity available to them AND add an additional three billion to the grid AND achieve no net growth in carbon output by 2050? Are we up against an impossible challenge?

Here's the other dimension to the challenge: carbon is emitted everywhere. It's belches from the smoke stacks of power plants, from the flares at refineries, from leaks in the natural gas transmission system, from every gasoline and diesel powered vehicle tailpipe, from factories, from your home heating ventilation and air conditioning (HVAC) unit, from cows farting, from peat melting in warming tundra, from organic material decomposing, and many, many other sources.

Wherever and whenever something is burned or organic matter decomposes, carbon is discharged. Anywhere fossil fuels or other raw materials are extracted, transported, or burned, carbon is being emitted. Anywhere organic material is decomposing, it is decomposing to carbon dioxide (eventually). And every product you buy has a carbon footprint attached to it.

While the premise of this book is that more than half of the carbon problem comes from electricity production and consumption and transportation needs, the truth is that rising levels of carbon in the atmosphere are a result of *rising levels of consumption*—consumption of *everything*, whether it is electricity for AC, plastic packaging, gasoline, food, or social media. Just think of the carbon emitted to collect and recycle glass, paper, and plastics, especially low-density plastic!

Carbon dioxide, methane, and other so-named greenhouse gases, are the byproducts of our Industrial Age, modern lifestyles, and national economies dependent on buying and consuming stuff. There are two broad solution sets for dealing with this:

1.  Collect all the carbon and put it somewhere, such as with carbon capture and sequestration (usually underground storage), recycle it, or render it inert,

2.  Avoid producing the carbon in the first place and consuming stuff that has carbon as a byproduct.

Solution set 1 is simply not practical. It is cost-prohibitive, and/or is subject to catastrophic release of the stored carbon. Think of a fire extinguisher; it's a carbon dioxide blanket designed to reduce the oxygen fanning the flames of a fire. A catastrophic release of $CO_2$ would displace the $O_2$ we breathe just like the fire extinguisher displaces the oxygen feeding the fire. Is that a risk we want to take?

This is why, I believe, solution set 2 is the only sensible way to meet the IPCC goal of zero net new carbon discharges by 2050. We must transform our economy from one dependent on fossil fuels to one served by low and carbon-free energy and we must reward people for consuming less stuff, thereby reducing their individual carbon footprints and driving change throughout the entire consumption-based economy. And, since electricity production and transportation make up more than half of the carbon discharge problem, we must fundamentally change these two sectors.

To reiterate: Today everything about our economic well-being depends on consumers buying stuff. The more stuff we buy, the larger carbon footprint we create. But, if all of us quit purchasing stuff, within days or weeks, tens of millions of people would be unemployed. So the seminal challenge is to create a new economic system that rewards people for consuming less!

The Carbon IRA is a great place to start, but it's only half the story when it comes to transforming our electricity and transportation systems. The other half is the YouTility concept, the subject of the second half of this book.

Back when I wrote that rant in *Lights Out!*, I implored the electricity industry to push innovation faster. At the time (April 2007), the industry was confronting multiple challenges, not the least of which were extraordinarily high prices for natural gas (the dominant source for electricity generation), escalating electricity prices, terrorist threats around the globe, and later that year, the global financial crisis.

One of my questions in that chapter was: *Where is the visionary company with the foresight and courage to lead the electricity industry into the low-carbon future and "pull" others along?* Ten years later, only one company has emerged, but, unfortunately, it's not an "electricity industry" company. It's an automotive company.

Without mentioning any names, (this is a big-picture concept book, after all) this company—let's call it Company A—is the only company I'm aware of that is pursuing the three pillars of the low carbon electricity future.

Specifically, it is:

1. Aggressively manufacturing, marketing, and selling electric vehicles (EV),
2. Developing and selling grid-scale and home-scale battery storage units, and
3. Supplying and installing rooftop solar photovoltaic (PV).
4. Plus, on top of all of that, the company is a leader in automation, self-driving cars, and digital and wireless control systems.

In other words, Company A has all of the pieces in place for the low-carbon, distributed energy, digital electricity future, but it does not have the decades of experience, nor the intimate understanding of how the electricity/utility industry differs from the sectors it has heretofore been participating in. Nevertheless, Company A is the one enterprise pursuing all aspects of the YouTility vision. It is putting enormous pressure on the traditional players in electricity and transportation.

But if we are to meet our net-zero carbon goals, we need many more visionary companies willing to lead so that we can transform our *moremoremore* consumption economy into a *think: less / think: smart* lifestyle.

So let's turn to the YouTility section of this little tome to see how it dovetails with the Carbon IRA framework to *address climate change and reward carbon reduction before it's too late.*

# YOUTILITY
## PART II

# YOUTILITY

Carbon IRA is about incentivizing the behaviors and consumer choices that reduce carbon footprint. YouTility is about creating a frame for the most important of those behaviors.

Climate change debates are often about complication and obfuscation. But here's one of the simplest things you'll ever need to know about reducing carbon footprint. Mitigating three-fifths of the problem can be accelerated immediately.

Here's why: Roughly one-third of the carbon output of the USA occurs from electricity production, today still predominantly by fossil fuel-fired power plants. While the percentage of coal in the mix is shrinking, it is being displaced largely by gas-fired power plants. That's a good thing, but modern gas-fired plants represent only about a

30 percent reduction in carbon compared to coal, whereas solar and wind are near zero, (if you account for life-cycle carbon in manufacturing and delivering wind turbines and PV systems).

Another nominal 30 percent of the carbon output occurs from the transportation sector, personal and commercial vehicles, also dependent almost exclusively on petroleum-derived products.

If our electricity production came from non-carbon sources—solar, wind, and other renewables (geothermal, hydroelectric), and nuclear power—and if the vehicles we drive were electric, the majority of the carbon-induced climate change calamity would be addressed!

Problem solved! Oh, if the world were so simple.

But in this case, it almost IS that simple, even if we'll need a decade or two to fully make the transition. The fact is that the products and technologies for renewable energy systems, large-scale electric storage batteries, and electric vehicles are fully developed, reasonably mature, and waiting to replace our fossil fuel-based infrastructure.

In fact, they already are, but not at a pace that will allow us to catch up with the ticking twelve-year climate change clock. The missing piece of the puzzle is the groundswell in consumer demand that will drive the economies of scale in the supply chains and drastically reduce prices.

I've been involved with electricity industry technologies for four decades. The only things preventing every single home and building in America from having solar PV on the roof, in an empty field, or other location are the capital cost of installing the system and the variability of the resources.

The only things preventing every one of those solar PV systems from being coupled with a large battery as backup for when the sun doesn't shine and the wind doesn't blow are the cost of the battery, the small amount of technical risk still present in batteries, and the immaturity of the battery sector as an industry.

And frankly, the reason there's not a surge in demand for these systems is that the electricity industry stakeholders—utilities, public utility commissions, system suppliers, etc.,—are arguing about how much money will be made and who is going to make it.

You probably buy electricity from your electric utility. Almost everyone does. If you are like me, you might have some solar panels on your roof. But you still need the utility for most of your electricity. But because the battery and solar systems technology and products are ready, your relationship with your utility *could be reversed!*

*You* could be producing most of the electricity you need from your own solar panels, storing what you can in a home-sized battery, and paying the utility for the small incremental amount you need every day to meet your peak demand, or in an emergency if your systems are down.

Today, your utility perceives that as an existential threat. If lots of people did it, the utility would charge everyone an inordinate amount of money for the back-up emergency power and the trickle they might need to keep up with daily demand.

It doesn't end with solar PV and battery storage, though. Every utility can add solar and wind facilities to their electricity grids. Every home can be designed today to be highly efficient ("smart" homes) and equipped with solar and storage. And, every personal vehicle can use that carbon-free electricity.

We just have to change the way we think about producing and consuming electricity, get rid of the institutional barriers standing in our way, and get that economic feedback loop spinning!

## THE VALUE CHAIN

At this point, it's helpful to have an understanding of our electricity grid infrastructure before we explain how it should be changed. Before electricity is delivered to a home or business, it is first generated in a power plant by converting an energy source into electricity. Then the electricity is fed through long transmission lines into distribution circuits, which then branch out and connect to every commercial building, school, church, community center, and residence, i.e. every consumer/ratepayer.

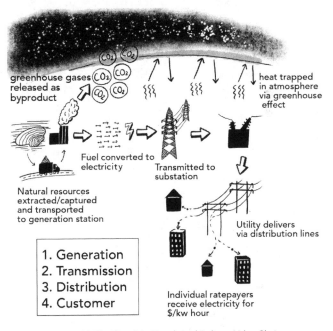

Figure 18. The Electricity Supply and Delivery Value Chain

Most of the power plants in the US convert a fossil fuel, coal or natural gas, into steam and then into electricity.

Around 15 percent of the power comes from nuclear, and around 15 percent is renewable, and most of that is hydro or wind. For a fossil fuel power plant, 60-80 percent of the cost of generating that electricity is for fuel. Today, only 9 percent of the country's electricity is generated by solar and wind. The beauty of solar and wind is three-fold:

1. It is carbon free, the attribute everyone focuses on.
2. The "fuel" is free, the attribute everyone *should* focus on a lot more! Raw solar and wind energy cost nothing.
3. Solar and wind require no water. Next to agriculture, fossil fuel-fired and nuclear power plants are together the second largest industrial consumers of water.

That said, there are also two major challenges with solar and wind:

1. The conversion of the energy into electricity is not very efficient, although this isn't so important when you are not paying for the "fuel."
2. The availability of the solar and wind energy is not guaranteed. The sun doesn't always shine and the wind doesn't always blow.

A fossil fuel or nuclear plant can generate electricity 24/7 for days and even months on end without interruption. (Some nukes can run for over a year without shutting down.) Obviously, solar can't make electricity at night, and is subject to cloud cover during the day. Wind has a problem on top of that. Often, the wind is strongest at night when the need for electricity is lowest. But these challenges are not insurmountable because grid-scale electricity storage helps to address the intermittency problem.

In fact, the advantages of renewable energy over fossil fuels are monumental and go beyond what I've described here. Imagine not having to dig any more coal out of the ground or pump natural gas from beneath the earth's surface. By itself, that saves a tremendous amount of energy, and avoids carbon discharges.

Also, although it's seldom included in the discussions, digging coal out of the ground releases methane. Tapping wells for natural gas and then transporting that fuel to where it is consumed also leaks methane. The volumetric amounts are relatively small. But here's the rub: Methane is around twenty times more potent than carbon dioxide in the atmosphere as a warming agent. In other words, a small percentage of leakage leads to a large impact on climate.

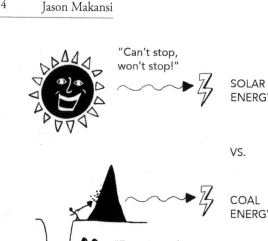

Figure 19. Energy from the sun vs. energy from dinosaur poop

Renewable energy sources avoid *all* of that.

The other beauty of solar in particular is that it can be installed wherever it makes the most sense. The same advantages accrue whether you put solar PV on 50 million roofs or build hundreds of utility-scale solar power facilities where the solar incidence is greatest and you transmit the electricity to where it is needed.

Yes, you lose system efficiency when you have to transmit electricity long distances; but again, the "fuel" is free. And, you can build and locate utility-scale battery facilities much like you would substations which connect transmission systems with electricity distribution circuits. Or, you can install millions of little storage units at individual buildings and homes.

*You become the utility!*

Because solar panels and storage can be installed wherever there is solar energy incidence, every home and building owner can supply much of their own electricity, in theory anyway.

When you combine this capability with new home automation devices, designed to minimize the amount of electricity consumed, such as state-of-the-art HVAC and energy efficient appliances, LED lighting, and intelligent building design, it becomes clear that you only really need an "outside" utility for what we call standby and peak power. And frankly, you might be able to cover this amount with a storage unit.

Electric utilities around the country realize this. They know that their most recent investments in big power plants and long transmission lines could be "stranded" (rendered unprofitable) if their ratepayers decide to become "YouTilities."

That's why they are fighting with environmental groups, utility commissions, digital firms, and other stakeholders. It's not that they are opposed to this transition to carbon-free, fuel-free, water-free electricity; they just want to control the speed at which the transition occurs. They want their figurative foot on the industry's gas (or brake) pedal, not someone else's.

I think the best and fastest way to satisfy everyone *and* beat the 12-year IPCC clock, is to allow utilities to invest in renewable-based distributed energy infrastructure, own the equipment on the roofs, the inverter and storage unit on the side of the house, and the electric vehicle hook-up in the garage, and let them earn their traditional regulated rate of return on the investments.

If you let a utility be the utility for the distributed energy future, then you need fewer YouTilities doing their own thing. The utilities are in the best position to manage the two-way flows of electricity between customers and the grid. But *advocating* for the YouTility framework will put necessary pressure on them to adapt sooner rather than later.

Personally, I'd rather reap all the benefits of this transformation without having to own or be responsible for the equipment. I think most people will feel the same. What people want are the lifestyle benefits of electricity without the carbon discharge and water consumption putting the planet—and the creatures, including humans, that depend on it—in peril.

## MORTGAGES AND ELECTRICITY

I estimate that for an average home in America, it would take $50,000 to be equipped as a "YouTility." That would include all the solar PV you could possibly put on the roof or the property, the largest battery storage unit, an electric car charging station, smart automation, energy-efficient appliances, etc. I also add in the difference in initial cost between an EV and a comparable gasoline-powered vehicle. Designed right, the huge car battery can help balance the supply and demand for the home.

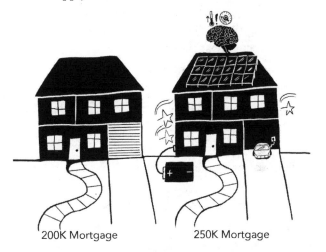

Figure 20. A Utility vs. a YouTility home and mortage

Unfortunately, very few people have fifty thousand dollars just sitting around to invest in being a "YouTility."

Since these are long-term investments, just like the house itself, why not roll up this capital investment into standard mortgages? The difference in monthly payment would be modest and you'd make it up on lower electricity rates. Landlords can finance YouTility upgrades for apartment buildings and multi-unit dwellings like they would finance any other major improvement and add the differential cost to the monthly rent, while charging less for electricity month to month.

Now, calculate the incentive payments deposited to long-term Carbon IRA retirement funds, and you begin to see the overall financial (and environmental) benefit for making these transformative choices.

## CUSTOMER CHOICE–THE PRIVATE SECTOR DEFINITION

Many private sector companies have bastardized the use of the word "choice," as in customer choice. Utilities have been studying, evaluating, and standing in the way of choice for decades. Way back in 2002, I wrote extensively about customer choice in electricity services in my first industry book, *An Investor's Guide to the Electricity Economy*.

Let's be clear: When electric utilities today laud their customer choice programs, they are referring to broad programs, cleared by their PUCs for investment recovery, in which the same "choice" is given to all customers in a certain rate class.

That choice, for example, goes something like this: We (the utility) will install a smart thermostat in your home, you can "choose" to run your AC less during the utility's peak demand period (a few hours during the hottest days of the summer) and we will reward you by sharing in the savings from your willingness to do that.

Another common choice is to select from one of several rate plans. You can choose to remain with the basic rate you've always had, which will be the higher of the options because it guarantees that you pay one rate with no limit on how much electricity you use. Or you can sign on to what's called a peak shaving rate where you pay a higher rate during the utility's peak demand periods, but a lower rate during off-peak hours. You can save money by (1) running your electricity intensive appliances (e.g., electric dryer) during off-peak hours, (2) reducing your AC and other electricity consuming devices during the high-priced peak periods.

Some of these choices may carry stiff penalties if you exceed a usage limit during the peak period. What the utility has typically done is gone from offering a "take it or leave it" rate structure (we're all bozos on the same bus) to offering you a few options for optimizing your usage with pricing. It's like going from no choice to basic A, B, or C choices—you want to sit at the front of the bus, the middle of the bus, the back of the bus?

These choices are a start, and I'm not arguing against them at all. What I'm advocating, though, is similar to the old adage, walk a mile in a person's shoes. Instead of persistently trying to change the electricity infrastructure by looking at it from the utility side of things, come to where I live and work (or apartment or office building or store, or factory, etc.) and look at it from the other direction! It sounds lame, but a change in scenery is always refreshing! And enlightening. And technology today enables utilities the opportunity to understand each customer and offer more customized choices. One size fits all is in the past, and even if you get to choose where to sit on the bus, you're still on a bus.

## CUSTOMER-CENTRIC CHOICES

The truth is, there are almost an infinite array of choices the ratepayer could make about his or her electricity consumption and infrastructure. And if we're going to make the rapid transition to a low-carbon electricity system and beat the climate clock, these choices must be confronted.

I began thinking long and hard about the YouTility concept when I moved from St. Louis to Tucson three years ago. We moved from a large, 100-year-old, two-story home to a smaller, single-story home that came with solar panels added ten years ago.

Tucson is a solar-rich area, and I began to wonder why the local utility didn't call on every new resident to discuss electricity options? I could have taken some of the money we made on the St. Louis house and invested it in additional solar panels, a smart thermostat system, a storage unit, a replacement for my inefficient HVAC unit (which dates to the year before the flood), LED lighting, and all kinds of other infrastructure. Instead, I'm greeted with a Welcome Wagon-type basket with coupons for buying stuff I don't need or want.

In other words, the utility needs to start reimagining the electricity ecosystem for each individual customer. And if the utility isn't willing to do that, then maybe one of the big digital automation firms needs to do it instead.

As electricity users, we must do our part to reimagine our electricity consumption and infrastructure, too. It's no longer about paying a little more or a little less for electricity each month. It's about survival.

Beating the climate change clock will take more than running your dishwasher at night. It will take a dynamic partnership between utility and ratepayer, mortgage company and underwriter, home builders, and commercial building developers, government agencies and environmental advocates, and everyone in between. Everyone. *We all need to get involved and get engaged because we are all part of the problem.*

## CONSUMER PRODUCTS MENTALITY

In my YouTility presentations, I use milk as an example of a consumer product we can all relate to. When I was a kid, my mother chose from basically three kinds of milk—whole, 2%, and skim. And forty years before that, there was probably one choice—what came out of the cow's teat (pasteurized, of course).

Today, there are three refrigerated shelves 12 feet long

Figure 21. Cow's milk used to dominate. Now there are many more choices.

with choices for milk, including: whole, 2%, 1%, skim, organic, non-organic, GMO, non-GMO, locally produced, regionally produced, nationally produced, almond, coconut, oat, and even milk produced from peas!

Every time I stand before consumer products shelves in a grocery big box store, I think about my friend who had a visitor from Soviet Russia in the early 1980s, who visited an American grocery store and was visibly frozen in place when she had to contemplate all the choices for soap.

In the Soviet Union, there was either soap or no soap! The choices our electric utilities give us today would probably be familiar to anyone from the old USSR!

And there are almost an infinite variety of choices for a no-carbon future. If the utility wants to install centralized renewable electricity generation and large scale storage, it could sign up ratepayers by offering the Carbon IRA benefit. This would be a clever way to retain customers and keep competition at bay.

New home builders can finance homes with all the YouTility bells and whistles rolled in, distinguish themselves in the market, and sell them at a premium. Or here's an alternate way to accomplish the same thing: Say a large home builder is developing a 250-unit subdivision. It could put solar on all the roofs, and supplemental electricity generation with a microgrid (a micro-utility system) that serves just the subdivision.

That microgrid could partially finance itself by selling electricity into the grid when the prices are best, and enhance the resiliency of the overall grid.

Some customers may have different attitudes about having electricity every minute of their lives, or how much air conditioning they need on really hot days, or whether they'd be willing to drastically reduce consumption during peak periods and be rewarded with a financial incentive or pay lower rates.

Figure 22. A neighborhood microgrid with solar energy

For example, I keep my thermostat at 81°F in the summer. For many people, that's intolerable. And I live in Tucson, AZ where it can get to 112°F in the shade. I might even be willing to risk a number of hours every summer where the thermostat is set at 85°F—if I were financially rewarded. I should be offered that option.

Because I can tolerate heat in the summer, I could also install an AC system that most people might consider "undersized." Why have an AC unit that can get the house down to 72°F, when I would never run it that way?

A smaller HVAC unit would reduce the cost of the home.

Figure 23. An average thermostat

Suppose I decide I can tolerate an AC system at 85°F most days of the summer? I can do this because I've got portable units working nearby that cool the space locally where I spend most of my time, like at my desk with my computer. I should be able to customize my usage if I want to because there is so much technology and there are so many products available that I can integrate and combine them to create a home electricity ecosystem that suits me and my family.

Unfortunately, HVAC suppliers prefer to sell a relatively small selection of models, and most companies that supply lighting and appliances, etc., are the same way. So the customer sees only the relatively few models that can be made at low cost through large-scale, assembly-line manufacturing.

Also, unlike industry veterans like me who think about power generation, transmission, and delivery and their ancillary products on a regular basis, the vast majority of people don't want to think about electricity at all. They just want to flip on a switch and enjoy the modern lifestyle it provides. Unfortunately, given the environmental damage our past choices have caused, we can no longer afford to be disengaged. We have to actively reimagine our relationship to the electricity that powers modernity, and we might as well reimagine a future that will benefit the environment, address climate change, and, coupled with Carbon IRA, put a few dollars in our pockets in the process!

## THE CASE FOR LOCAL CONTROL

When we lived in St. Louis, our house was relatively large—4,000 square feet—and was zoned for separate cooling on both floors. We could manage the "local" temperature depending on what part of the house we were using. Sounds smart, right? Unfortunately, the thermostat downstairs on the first floor was located in the main hall so that when the front door opened and a blast of cold winter or hot summer air flowed in, it flowed right past the thermostat. And, when my wife wanted to use the gas fireplace in the family room, that room got extra cozy, the thermostat registered the increased temperature, and the rest of the first floor became an icebox.

Here in Tucson, I recently moved my office from an extra room at the front of the house (adjacent to the guest bedroom) into the rather spacious master bedroom. After my wife heads to work in the morning, I spend most of my day in this one room, even though we live in an 1,800 square foot house. Clearly, heating and cooling the entire house as if I am going to be hanging out in the other rooms is wasteful.

A smarter approach would be to equip each section of the house, including the master bed/bath/office, with a local HVAC capability and keep the rest of the house at commensurate higher or lower temperature. Many homes already have "smart" zoning, but because of inefficient design or particular preferences, we often resort to adding ceiling fans, space heaters, small room air conditioners, or even stand-up or desk fans to address local comfort.

But there are ways to more efficiently control "local" temperature while optimizing energy use. While I'm at my desk, for instance, I could use a chair equipped with a thermoelectric heating and cooling capability set to maintain my particular preferences. Ditto for the mattress, or I could use a heating and cooling blanket set to my preferred temperature. In time, we could be wearing clothes woven with thermoelectric threads and powered by rechargeable battery packs.

The point is that it is imperative that we re-imagine our electricity use *now*. And new thinking about highly localized comfort should be part of the overall infrastructure equation. Further, it is imperative that we *accelerate* the transformation from an antiquated fossil fuel-based electricity grid and petroleum-based transportation system. The ultimate outcome is to dramatically reduce carbon discharges for which the electricity and transportation sectors, and by extension ratepayers and vehicle owners and operators—you and I—are responsible.

Millions have been spent on policy proposals, high-level assessments, carbon trading markets, environmental regulations, and many other parts of the solution. But no one has proposed a framework that involves financially incentivizing the behavior changes necessary to reach our carbon-avoidance goals by coupling those changes with saving for the future. The Carbon IRA coupled with YouTility-type thinking is the game-changing accelerant we need to beat the clock on climate change.

## BYE BYE LANDLINE

The YouTility concept forces us to reverse our thinking on how electricity is supplied and delivered. For more than 100 years, the paradigm has been that a large quasi-governmental entity, a utility, is responsible for providing electricity and its considerable lifestyle benefits to everyone. That has been the goal. *To everyone.*

The problem with this paradigm today is that the utility confronts the same existential threats that AT&T confronted thirty years ago when wireless cell phone technology was advancing faster than AT&T could adapt. The benefits of cell phones surpassed the ability of the largest communications monopoly to control how the technology would be rolled out to customers. Other companies stepped into the breach and transformed the telephone industry into the wireless communications industry—and transformed our lives in the process.

Today, renewable energy-based distributed energy technology poses an existential threat to the traditional utility business model. Each ratepayer can choose to be their own YouTility, and even sell electricity back to the grid. New companies are pushing these options to ratepayers, and a precious few utilities are even encouraging these programs. Before long, consumers will be able to quit paying for "the landline," in this case the cable that connects to the utility distribution grid and the services it provides.

I'm tempted to say that electricity ratepayers will probably never be able to sever that connection completely. But, I'll also bet that thirty years ago, AT&T (and the competitors which entered the business in the 1980s) never thought that phone customers would take that last drastic step and quit paying for the landline, the lifeline, the backup to the cellphones.

We now know otherwise. We have multiple ways and multiple devices with which to communicate.

For at least twenty years, I've listened to utility industry executives profess interest in becoming "customer-centric" businesses. Most of them have managed to do so for the industrial and commercial customers who buy significant quantities of electricity. Losing these customers presents immediate financial hardship for the utility.

Most utilities still think of the rest of us customers in the collective. We're just one big "customer." But I believe the utilities that continue this old way of thinking will face extinction.

Those utilities that take the time to understand each customer's needs and provide new apps, services, and distributed energy systems will thrive. Utilities are in the best position to offer advice and counsel to ratepayers about matching electricity infrastructure, rate plans, etc., to their specific needs. They are in the best position to invest in, own, operate, and maintain the distributed infrastructure and provide customized services and carbon-free electricity to customers.

But if they aren't willing to change, the collective is going to have to pressure them into it. Or some other company is going to step into the breach and offer those services instead.

## CHANGING THE PARADIGM

You can't blame your utility for being slow to change and for not rapidly embracing the distributed YouTility paradigm. This, after all, is their history.

The whole idea of supplying electricity was to offer a "vanilla" product to everyone, often subsidized by large industrial and commercial accounts to keep costs reasonable to the "average" household. It is, in many ways, a socialized service. Everyone pays into the system. Everyone benefits from it at some baseline equitable level.

To your utility, you are no different from your neighbor. You both get the same meter on the side of your house, the same rates and fees, and so on.

The YouTility framework unequivocally shifts the conversation and the paradigm from a centralized, paternal approach (we are the utility, we know what's best for you) to one where optimized electricity using infrastructure for an individual consumer ("Here's what I want. Can you provide it?") is at the center of the business.

Consumer products companies have long understood how to create product "platforms" which can be customized for individuals. This is why you are confronted with a dizzying array of options when you go to buy a new car, or cell phone, or even look at the soap shelves in the department store.

And like other consumer products, new options that enable individuals to customize their energy infrastructure means that this "every customer is the same" mentality cannot and will not last. It is already changing. It's just a matter of how fast. Advances in technology are accelerating the change, but we must also act as an accelerant.

I recently read an article about an apartment dweller who wanted to purchase an electric vehicle, but the lack of a charging station at his complex was a barrier. So he convinced the landlord to install one for $8,000 on the assumption that it would be a good investment for future tenants and a way to distinguish that apartment complex from the competition.

I believe that if electricity ratepayers were aware of all of the options available, they would similarly get engaged with their utility—and their landlords and builders and mortgage lenders, etc.—to advocate for and force changes.

And that is the purpose of this half of this book. Utilities are rightfully concerned about several things, though.

First, they have made investments in the centralized infrastructure—new power plants, long transmission lines, centralized solar facilities, wind farms, etc.—which are imperiled if customers install their own rooftop PV and battery storage systems. Second, the more intelligently and efficiently customers manage their electricity consumption, the less revenue for the utility.

In truth, though, the displacement of gasoline-powered vehicles by electric ones will not only increase the need for electricity generation capacity, it will also "balance" that need between the daytime hours and nighttime hours.

Think about it: Very little electricity is consumed at night when everyone is asleep and workers are at home. Something similar happens between weekdays and weekends, and between summer, winter, spring, and fall. We call these daily, weekly, and seasonal peak loads.

Migration to EVs actually improves an electric utility's demand profile. Most EV charging would take place at night, and assets in place to serve the day's peak could be operated to meet this increase in nightly load thereby enhancing the asset's productivity.

In truth, it's the petroleum industry that is threatened by EVs, not electric utilities! But don't feel sorry for them either. When they finally sense the seismic shift to EVs, they will simply invest in the electricity industry or acquire the appropriate companies. I've been watching them do this since I got my first job in the industry.

It's not change these behemoth oil and electricity companies are afraid of—it's *losing control* over that change!

## OUTCOMES ARE COMPELLING

Three years after buying a home equipped with solar panels, I love the fact that those panels sit up there generating electricity when the sun shines. They require no maintenance. The surfaces don't even need to be washed. The intermittent rains in Tucson take care of that.

It's a portentous coincidence that I purchased a solar-powered home now that I'm on the cusp of retirement, because when I started my career, I worked in huge coal-burning power stations. Although today, many of those facilities are automated and fewer staff are employed, back then they required hundreds of expert craft workers and dozens of engineers on site to operate and maintain the equipment.

In contrast, solar PV just sits there. There's no rotating equipment, no engines, no conveyor belts, no large boilers with huge flames, no pulverizers, or emissions control equipment, no piping with dangerous fluids at high pressure and temperature flowing through them, no acres of filthy staging areas for train cars delivering coal mined thousands of miles away, no cooling ponds, and no smokestacks equipped with scrubbers and other pollution control equipment. Just panels, wiring, and an inverter to convert the DC power to AC for the distribution circuit.

Even large wind farms with hundreds of turbine/generators are operated remotely and must be maintained by a roving staff responsible for thousands of individual turbines. Solar PV, on the other hand, requires almost zero regular maintenance, especially compared to all other options for generating electricity.

You know what else is zero for solar PV? Water consumption! Traditional power plants require *huge* amounts of water for cooling and that has to be treated (in an expensive process) for the feed water that is converted to steam.

So, in addition to the zero carbon footprint, there are negligible operations and maintenance (O&M) costs (relatively speaking) and zero water consumption. It's a win on carbon emissions, a win on operations, a win on maintenance, and a win on water use.

In fact, distributed solar PV + storage (batteries) so profoundly alters the economics of electricity, you have to wonder why we aren't all demanding a national imperative to get as much of it installed as quickly as possible. It boggles the mind. I mean we are talking about:

- Zero marginal carbon emissions
- Zero fuel costs
- Zero marginal labor costs, and
- Near zero costs for operations and maintenance compared to other generation options.

But, we are also talking about an existential threat to utilities: *zero marginal need for the utility to supply our electricity.*

ZERO marginal carbon
ZERO marginal labor
ZERO marginal cost
ZERO marginal need for a centralized grid

(Marginal refers to the next increment of kW capacity or kWh consumed)

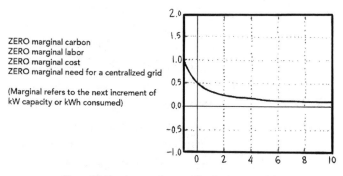

Figure 24. The threat to the prevailing business model

## SUBSIDIES AND INCENTIVES

What makes all this even more complex is that there are federal and (in some locations) state and local subsidies and incentives to help me (and you) make investments to install solar PV. There are also "green" loan programs, clean energy financing, and energy efficiency home loan programs available. And there are, currently, federal tax breaks for buying EVs and solar PV, and some utilities are required to provide additional incentives.

The problem is not enough effort is made to expose consumers to all these programs and help them think through their options.

To reap the benefits of YouTility, the distributed infrastructure has to be considered in a holistic way. Just adding a "smart" thermostat isn't going to do much, even if the utility has a program to help you install it.

Every home is different, and every person living in it is different. Some people are home all day. Some are home only a few hours. Some people tolerate cold poorly and heat well (me!); others, (like my wife), are the opposite. For some people, an EV's 200-300-mile range is fine. For others, it is not okay.

Until you invest the time to understand the personal needs and then match the infrastructure to those needs, distributed energy is going to advance slowly and the traditional centralized architecture will remain entrenched.

YouTility (coupled with Carbon IRA) is intended to disrupt the status quo and accelerate the rate of change.

## YOUTILITY AT THE APP STORE

In my YouTility presentations, I talk a lot about smart phones. While some "Smart Home" apps are already available, they need to be more widespread, intuitive, easy to use—and affordable. I should be able to open the app on my phone and see an array of monitoring and control options for my electricity infrastructure.

Figure 25. Someday you'll be able to get a smart home interface in the ap store

**Rooftop solar**—My solar PV inverter and utility meter should report how many kilowatt-hours are being produced, how much I am buying from or selling to the utility, the conversion efficiency of the panels (so I would know if the surfaces needed to be cleaned), and so on. All of this data is (or could be) reported to the company which installed the solar PV so it can monitor its health and performance. Why shouldn't I have these data, too?

**HVAC**—It should be simple to program my thermostat for settings appropriate for different periods of the day and for the different rooms I spend time in. I should also be able to monitor how much power the HVAC is drawing and easily reset the temperatures. And I should be able to lower the temperature to reduce power draw (and carbon output) remotely and turn the temperature back up before I arrive home.

**Appliances**—I should be able to load my dishwasher, have it programmed to turn on at 1:00 a.m. (when electricity rates are lowest, and if I am on a peak/off-peak rate plan). And I should also be able to reset the time it will turn on if, for example, I remember that I need clean beer mugs ready before friends arrive to watch the afternoon game.

I can communicate with my cloud backup file storage system from anywhere with internet access, so why shouldn't I be able to comunicate with my appliances, too?

**Lighting**—I should be able to return home, hit a button to turn on additional outside lights while I am turning onto my street, and then turn off all the lights in the home when I retire for the evening. My smart phone "lighting app" should show me a diagram with all of the lights, which ones are on or not, and a 'switch" so I can individually turn them off and on.

**Electric vehicle**—If charged up, EVs with large batteries should be able to serve as emergency backup when service from the utility or solar PV is disrupted (during a storm, for example). And if the EV is charged up using solar PV, it could feed that solar (carbon-free) electricity into the YouTility when it isn't being used. And I should be able to monitor all of this on my app.

**Carbon IRA**—All of my carbon-free kilowatt hours and my carbon-free vehicle miles should be monitored, tallied, and exported to my Carbon IRA app, which, in turn, will monitor and display how much money has been credited to my account.

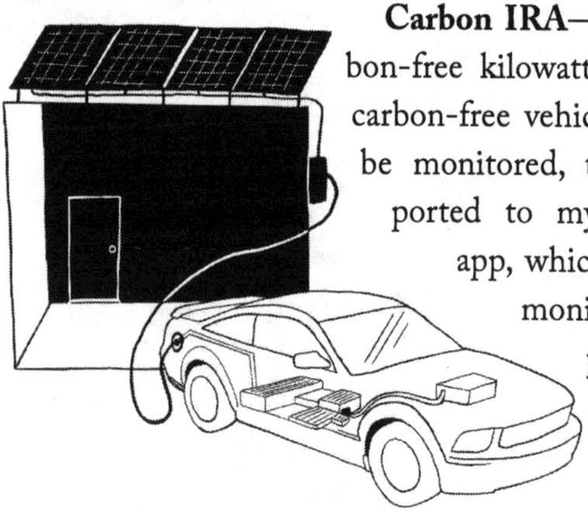

Figure 26. Electric vehicle charged by solar power

With real-time information, I could also make decisions like sell my carbon-free KWhs to the utility during peak periods, sacrifice some AC comfort, and/or accrue additional funds in my account.

Every dollar someone saves is the result of a choice not to spend that dollar today. We need to think of our carbon footprint in the same way. Just imagine if a utility made up for the revenue it would lose when I become a YouTility by managing my avoided carbon just like a bank!

The only thing different from what you can do today is that I am substituting electricity for some other product or service. We can monitor our credit card statements, bank accounts, and investment from our smart phones. We can access virtually and immediately the knowledge of the world through the internet.

The technology needed to implement the Carbon IRA & YouTility framework is available and getting more sophisticated every day. Technology isn't the problem. Will and determination and demand are.

For instance, for those who can afford them, the most advanced EVs are a dream to drive. The traditional automotive dashboard has been replaced with a large computer screen that acts as an internet interface, a navigation device, search engine, and portal for exchanging information with the car company in real-time. The computer tells the driver everything they need to know about that vehicle, including all maintenance information and software updates, where the nearest charging stations are, and how long charging will take. The computer knows where the car is located at all times and a connected app allows for real-time remote tracking. There is an option for the car to drive itself, and the driver can text or call hands-free at any time. Plus the vehicle has a breathtaking sound system which allows the driver to access all the music the world has to offer and play it on speakers that are absolutely divine.

Meanwhile, some cars more than a few years old (including our old car) don't even have a plug to play tunes from an iPhone. And (almost) every non-EV on the road runs on carbon-spewing gasoline that has to be refined from a fossil fuel pumped out of the ground and then transported by tanker truck to the local filling station.

Why aren't more people demanding more EVs from every automaker?

And most utilities offer only a basic peak/off-peak rate plan and limited smart home connectivity. Why aren't more people demanding more options and services from their utilities?

When is my utility (or some company willing to disrupt the utility model) going to send me a postcard with an offer to install and finance an EV charging station, rooftop solar PV, and a comprehensive, smart home control and monitoring station accessible from my smart phone?

I'm ready.

Are you?

## MOVING IN THE RIGHT DIRECTION

Not all electric utilities are as lame as the ones in the places I've lived. Some are already moving in the right direction, but need a nudge. Let me describe what I believe the most forward looking utility in our business is doing.

First, understand that the foundation for YouTility, and the home utility app vision I laid out above isn't hardware per se, but data. *Lots of data*. And the ability to collect and manage data automatically.

Many utilities benefited from an Obama-era program that subsidized the installation of smart meters at ratepayer facilities across the service territory. These meters are data gold mines.

They also serve as the basis for what the industry calls "demand-side management (DSM) programs." Simply put, if you get a customer to avoid a kilowatt-hour of usage, that's a kilowatt hour of production avoided, too. The trick is to make the customer's behaviors as predictable as possible. When you invest in reducing demand, you avoid investment in power plants and transmission lines.

Key to making DSM work in the case of this forward-looking utility was to install two-way thermostats in lots of homes. The thermostats are really data recorders and transmitters. They take data every 15-minutes which are then plugged into a model that calculates energy consumption patterns specific to each home. The model creates a "comfort profile" for each home.

A smart phone interface accompanies each smart thermostat. The executive of this utility rightly noted that, because the interface competes, in the mind of the customer, with retailers and other apps on the phone, it better be "comparable." Thus, the utility understands that the future competition is probably digital firms, not other utilities.

Each thermostat can be remotely controlled by the utility to help balance demand with production, especially on hot days. Customers who participate in the program allow the utility to automatically adjust the temperature setting and cycle their AC units on and off for short periods of time during an "event." An event is described as when peak demand approaches the utility's ability to meet that demand. This occurs during the afternoons between May and September in the utility's region.

In essence, the largest consumer of electricity in the home, the AC unit, comes under the control of the utility, just like the power plants, transmission lines, and distribution circuits. This is certainly one way to achieve the YouTility vision, and probably, as I explained above, the most practical all the way around.

The utility supplies and installs the thermostats at no charge. It then shares some of the savings with the customer through a rebate program. The thermostat also monitors the performance of the HVAC system and can recommend maintenance tasks, like cleaning filters, or checking coolant levels.

The latest feature being rolled out is pre-cooling. The customer premises can be pre-cooled to dampen the effect of the rise in temperature during the curtailment event. This is more about shifting the demand than reducing it, however.

Solar PV and EV hook-ups are going to be added to the program in time. The utility also partnered with a home builder to construct close to 200 LEED (Leadership in Energy and Environmental Design, the most widely used green building rating system) certified homes, each with 2 kW solar PV on the roof, demand responsive thermostats, and automated intelligent agents. Ten of these customer sites have 8 kWh batteries.

As for all that data being collected, the ratepayer will actually own the data, but the utility is the "steward" of it. Therefore, if the ratepayer moves, they can take their data with them and use it when setting up their new home system—if the new home has an advanced system, of course.

You can't even imagine the cultural transformation this required of the utility organization. For the last 100 years, the utility built large power plants, transmitted and distributed the electricity to customers, and billed them. This is radically different from *avoiding* the need for 200 MW of electricity by actively controlling infrastructure in each home hour by hour. Different still will be installing, monitoring, and controlling solar PV, and EV chargers at each home.

If electricity producers and consumers (all of us) are going to "get ahead" of our impact on climate change, we need to catalyze and accelerate transformations such as this.

## LET'S JUST GET ON WITH IT!

I fervently believe the fastest way to accelerate the transformation is to drive it from the customer end of the meter and force utilities and other participants to adapt to consumer demands.

I would rather that electricity ratepayers initiate an engagement en masse with their utility and see how far down the YouTility pathway each ratepayer can go. Today. *Now.*

It's a secondary or tertiary concern whether, as in the example above, the utility is in control of the distributed infrastructure in the home or building, or whether the homeowner/resident wishes to own and control it themself.

As for me, I want my utility to work with me. I want them to help me customize the infrastructure to my lifestyle, co-invest with me, own and maintain the infrastructure, and send me a bill every month. I don't want to be responsible for the equipment. I am almost always willing to pay for expertise and convenience. I just want the service.

But not everyone is like me. My friend across town is a computer geek who just added massive solar PV to his roof. Right now, he drives a hybrid, but plans to replace it with an EV. He doesn't just want service. He wants to control it. He even built his own apps to monitor and track his solar energy and installed room AC units to optimize his cooling with his solar PV production. According to his son, he's been threatening to go "off grid" for years!

He's almost there.

Utilities that want to survive and be part of the solution instead of continuing to contribute to the problem and ultimately being disrupted right out of business, need to greet the existential threat of millions of ratepayers like my friend going "off grid" as an opportunity for transformation. And they need to put on their walking shoes and start knocking on doors and having conversations with customers about how they can help plan and manage every customer's YouTility.

## GETTING THE MONEY

We're a capitalist economy so getting the "capital" for such transformations is always an issue. Fortunately, there are plenty of options for financing and investing in the YouTility vision.

You'd be surprised at how many programs and subsidies might be available to you, depending on your location. The greatest surprise perhaps is why these programs are not more heavily promoted so people are aware of them.

Some states have "net metering" programs. Net metering means that the utility is obligated to buy the electricity from your rooftop solar PV, usually at an inflated price, and credit you for that electricity in your billing statement. They were early programs designed to encourage "early adopters" to make the solar PV decision and were heavily skewed in favor of ratepayers.

Most of these programs around the country have been scaled back so they are not so favorable to ratepayers. That's because they were over-subscribed and utilities could see the writing on the wall.

Many people take out home equity loans to refurbish a kitchen or bathroom. Why not do the same for electricity infrastructure? HUD and Fannie Mae offer reduced rate mortgages for so-called "smart" and energy-efficient homes. These and other "green bank" financing mechanisms were available under the Obama administration. Trump may have yanked them away, just like his administration is yanking away the tax incentives for EVs and solar PV.

A similar program is called "property assessed clean energy" (PACE) financing. This is a way to finance energy features with "societal benefits" through tax-advantaged property assessment schemes. One feature of these programs is that future residents of the property continue to pay for the investments you made through an elevated property tax. Some of the tax burden, in other words, is shifted to future residents since they will also benefit from the "social good" of less carbon.

Instead of purchasing rooftop solar PV with a single cash outlay, you can either finance the installation through the OEM who provides it or lease it. These are more complicated because a third party owns stuff that's on your roof. Plus, leasing terms often negate the financial advantages of reducing the utility bill.

Some utilities are beginning to offer (or are considering offering) a reduced electricity rate for a firm period of charging your EV. Utilities like to make demand as predictable as possible. It's less costly for them to supply ten thousand EV chargers with juice during a certain time period than it is to randomly supply ten thousand chargers whenever the ratepayer "plugs in."

And some states, often through utilities, offer subsidies and rebates for replacing old appliances with energy-efficient ones. All of these programs differ from utility to utility, from state to state, and from administration to administration. They tend to fluctuate with the prevailing political winds. This is why the YouTility framework has to integrate four aspects:

1. Financing, investment, and monthly servicing fees;
2. Homeowner/household lifestyle, comfort profiles, and aspirations;
3. Technological and product options;
4. Local regulatory and policy structures.

A key part of the customer's "aspirations" is the degree to which he/she wishes to be part of the climate change solution rather than the problem. A key part of the financing and investment is how much money they are willing to put where their mouth is.

An important aspect of the lifestyle and comfort dimension is a customer's attitude towards having electricity all of the time. This is a critical piece.

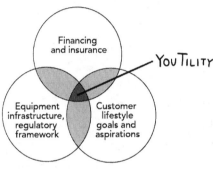

Figure 27. The elements of the YouTility framework

American utilities have always assumed that every customer wants electricity 24/7/365. That's why electricity grids are designed for 99.9 percent reliability. They are designed so that only a few outages occur each year and each outage only lasts from a few minutes to a few hours at most (except on rare occasions). Those who have visited countries where the electricity goes off at random times of the day and for random periods of time appreciate and depend upon the 24/7/365 reliability that powers modern life. But it is important to note that achieving this impressive level of reliability means that grids are designed with ample "reserve margin."

In most parts of the country, this reserve margin is from 15-25 percent of the peak demand, defined as the most electricity expected to be needed in any given hour or period for that year. Other industries would decry this—saying it is 20 percent overbuilt.

Suppose my kids' generation decided that they could manage with 98 percent reliability, or between 150 and 200 hours a year with no electricity? Suppose they were willing to make that sacrifice because their aspiration is to tread more lightly on the planet? Shouldn't they be rewarded for that, share in the savings that the utility would experience?

When we experienced a multi-day utility outage in St. Louis in the hottest part of the summer, my kids slept in the basement and hung out at a coffee shop which had power. As long as they were "connected," they were fine. Me? I went bonkers. I'd never gone more than a half a day without electricity unless I was (reluctantly) camping. But we managed.

Then there was that time my wife and I left the four year old and the baby with my mom, took off for a Caribbean resort, and hadn't even landed when a winter storm back home pulled the plug for almost 36 hours. It was a good thing we had a fireplace.

Some people today make obscene amounts of money renting their homes through Airbnb; sometimes, so much that they stay in a cheap motel while "guests" enjoy their place. And some use Uber or Lyft and don't even have a driver's license, let alone a car. Without generalizing too much, some in the younger generation have absolutely no interest in owning "their father's Oldsmobile." These young adults are likely to interact very differently with their electricity infrastructure. And they should be allowed the freedom to choose how they do so.

YouTility means designing a home electricty use profile and system for someone who can live with 98% reliability and doesn't own a car. It also means designing a home electricty use profile and system for someone who likes maximum AC in the summer, plenty of heat in the winter, doesn't live in a solar-advantaged area, and wants a truck, a minivan, and a convertible in their three-bay garage.

## ADDRESSING THE URGENCY

The technological innovation required to implement the Carbon IRA & YouTility vision is minimal. Solar PV is already affordable and effective. Grid-scale storage is getting affordable and just needs some fine-tuning to deliver commodity-level products and services.

The challenges center on political will and motivating individuals to change their behavior.

But let's return to the twelve-year countdown clock humanity is staring at, the point at which we could experience from 1.5-2.0°C average global temperature rise.

Figure 28. The Doomsday Clock - Twelve Years to Midnight

Twelve years. That's the time it takes for a newborn to become a pre-teen. Those of us who are parents know that's no time at all. And we're supposed to effect a global transformation in that time period? *How is this possible?*

For starters, let's take a page from history. Almost 140 years ago, Thomas Edison built the first centralized electricity generating station on Pearl Street in lower Manhattan, the Pearl Street station. By the early decades of the next century, private companies across America were vying to electrify urban areas, because the population density made it profitable to do so.

By the 1930s, more than 50 percent of the population had access to electricity, but the industry had by then evolved into just a few huge monopolies thereby corrupting the business, gouging consumers, duplicating infrastructure, and refusing to serve unprofitable rural areas.

Along with many of the political changes post-Great Depression, the electricity industry became regulated. Each "utility" was given a monopoly over a "service territory," and a public utility commission set consumer rates based on allowing a reasonable rate of return on invested capital.

Electricity was seen as something all citizens should have access to, and access was seen as a right, not a privilege. People were more productive people with lighting in buildings, and much more comfortable with air conditioning. Electricity not only powered the economy, it drove modernity, leading to healthier lifestyles, greater efficiencies (so people could spend their time on other things), revolutionary new technologies, etc. Electricity drove the explosive growth of whole industries, such as aluminum, copper, steel, and heavy manufacturing, which depend on consuming huge amounts of electric energy.

You can see how it all became a positive reinforcing feedback loop. Arguably, the golden age of regulated electric utilities lasted from the end of WWII to the late 1960s. Greater electrification spurred economic growth factors of 5-6 percent each quarter, nothing like the 2-3 percent economic growth we think of as healthy today.

In those three decades, electricity production and delivery infrastructure essentially tripled! It was built under the assumption that electricity was a social good, a lubricant for the economy, and a commodity that went from a luxury and convenience to a necessity. Living without electricity was considered backward, even life-threatening and unhealthy.

The US electricity miracle, or "grid," often described as the largest "machine" ever built, became a model for the rest of the world. Part of that miracle, by the way, was that an investment in utility stocks were some of the safest and most dependable investments people could make for their retirement or savings. They were called "stocks for widows and orphans"!

Why? Because the regulatory process guaranteed an 8-12 percent return on their investments so people who invested in them were similarly rewarded with predictable, steady returns. Things changed in the 1970s. OPEC-induced energy crises and poor legislative responses; cost overruns with nuclear power plants, wasteful practices, slowing economic growth, global economic competition, especially from the countries we rebuilt after WWII (Germany and Japan); and the grand neoliberal/

neoconservative deregulation experiments driven from academia and policy-making consultants were all factors.

For our purposes here, let's just skip over all that and return to what worked.

What worked is that the regulated utility business model was put into practice with an awesome and almost impossible-to-achieve goal: Deliver electricity to everyone! Within three decades, that goal had been achieved. It wasn't an emergency; it was desirable. It was a foundation for the rest of our economic growth and for everything that undergirds our modern lifestyles.

But today, we have an emergency! Today, we have to contend with the *unintended consequences* of electricity for all—its contribution to an average global temperature rise of 2-9°C by as early as the middle of this century caused by the carbon discharges of modernity.

*Yet, electricity is still the solution.*

We just have to transform how we produce it and consume it. And everyone who claims we have to return to the Dark Ages in order to address climate change either doesn't understand the electricity industry or is lying for political purposes. Because achieving the goal of no net carbon by the middle of the century doesn't depend on new technologies or nascent innovations. It depends on vision, foresight, and political will.

The US can and should again be the model for the rest of the world.

Every state, city, and municipal government in the country simply needs to decide and take action underpinning the idea that the new societal goal is to minimize carbon footprint as quickly as possible without sacrificing the benefits of electricity. To do that, they can further decide and take action to expand the definition of the infrastructure the utility can invest in to include every building—residential or commercial.

Municipal utilities already have the power to do this because they are owned by their city governments. Cooperative utilities are owned by their ratepayers so they just need to demonstrate the collective will. Investor-owned utilities just need a decree from their public utility commissions.

I guarantee you that if utilities are allowed to invest—in lieu of or along with investments by building owners—in rooftop solar PV, on-site storage units, electric vehicle charging infrastructure, centralized wind and solar power plants, offshore wind farms, transmission lines, and even energy-efficient appliances and advanced lighting in residential units, and earn an 8-12 percent return on their capital investments, they will be chomping at the bit to get started.

Here are the repercussions of the scenario I envision:

- Wall Street would be happy to push utility stocks and bonds as sound investments, raising even more funds.
- Utilities would immediately phase out their fossil fuel-burning power stations and replace them with fuel-free, carbon-free renewable sources.
- Storage units and electric vehicles would drop in cost rapidly as demand pushes more supply and competition, and the law of economies of scale takes hold.
- Demand in the US, the second largest economy in the world, would drive transformation in other countries.

One law is inexorable: Electricity from expensive fossil-fuel sources that have to be dug out of the ground, transported long distances, and then burned, cannot prevail economically against electricity from sources that are fuel-free, carbon-free, maintenance-free, and water-free.

Like I said earlier, I don't care if we get there with the YouTility framework or the Utility framework. We just need to get there, *post haste*. Plus, the Carbon IRA & YouTility fits neatly into the "Green New Deal," an umbrella term for the variety of programs being proposed by candidates across the political spectrum. The Obama administration started down this path with the American Reinvestment and Recovery Act (ARRA), which allocated large sums to support utilities in their "smart meter" programs; to create subsidies for solar, wind and electric vehicles; fast commuter train systems; and to advance electric energy storage from research and development to demonstration.

The Democratic-controlled House of Representatives in Obama's first two years passed a Carbon Cap and Trade bill, although it did not pass the Senate. That could be viewed as the last hurrah of the neo-liberals and conservatives who believed "market forces" could cure all economic ills in all situations (except when it came to the need for farm and oil/gas subsidies).

Now, the Green New Deal is a way to convert our energy infrastructure from fossil fuels to renewable sources, create millions of new jobs, and get down the path of cutting our carbon discharges in half by 2030. It ambitiously calls for obtaining 100 percent of our electricity from renewable sources in ten years.

The Green New Deal probably isn't achievable, and isn't meant to be. It's an organizing principle, a straw man that legislators and voters can chew on, pick apart, attack, consider, and work forward from. Some versions could include nuclear power as a carbon-free source. That's also okay with me, although the nuclear industry has, in the recent past, shown itself to be more than capable of shooting itself in both feet with one bullet.

Imagine how much more effective this restructuring will be if, going forward, consumers are rewarded for their carbon avoidance with funds for retirement! This time around, the unintended consequences of electricty industry restructuring could very well be healthier Americans (because they eat better and exercise more), lower costs for health care, consistent support for mass transportation systems, less stress on our social security system, and many other benefits.

Rather than imposing a huge new "command and control" bureaucracy to attempt to effect change, the federal government should simply:

1. Set the goals for the reduced carbon footprint,
2. Support the states and their PUCs in driving the needed regulatory changes, and
3. Motivate voters/consumers with retirement savings.

So instead of pushing another top-down program, they should offer permanent bottoms-up incentives consistent with the urgency of the twin challenges of destructive climate change and inadequate retirement funds, and use the historically successful institutional structure—the regulated utility—that is already in place, and that has worked well for decades. This is not rocket science. We can implement solutions commensurate with the urgency of the challenge. And we can do it starting now.

## MANAGING THE TECHNICAL RISKS

Here's another good thing about using the regulated utility model for getting infrastructure built in a hurry: It's a great way to manage both technological and business risk.

As I mentioned earlier, we don't need a lot of new innovation to build a distributed infrastructure that gets us to a carbon-free electricity system. But we do need some, in particular for the critical energy storage systems. The other area of risk is in scaling up (and out) the infrastructure. It's one thing for a small, upstart company to put a few thousand solar PV systems on residential rooftops. But it's quite another to scale that up to tens of thousands, even millions.

Companies with a new "widget" often get funding from the government for RD&D, critical to move them forward to commercialization. Unfortunately, most of these companies fail, although the good news is that the technology often continues under a larger, more stable company.

Regulated utilities are not known for their appetite for innovation. However, the regulated utility model has already shown that it is well-suited for rapid conversion of technologies on the cusp of commercialization to infrastructure-level capacities, and for getting large-scale infrastructure installed relatively quickly.

In the early 1990s, advanced gas turbine technology was at a similar point as energy storage—large new machines 50 percent more powerful than their predecessors had been demonstrated but not widely deployed. In less than a decade, which is a blink of the eye for building infrastructure, hundreds of these machines were in place and operating.

These machines have substantially displaced coal-fired power capacity, by the way, which has reduced the industry's carbon footprint considerably. Natural gas has less carbon than coal, and because these machines have a higher efficiency, the relative emissions for the same power output are commensurately lower.

The regulated utility model is ideal for a business that has to invest huge sums of money with a 20-50-year time horizon. It is designed to provide some level of protection so that new technologies at large scale can "mature" without the volatility that private sector firms are subjected to.

In other words, they don't have to answer to a quarterly earnings report, or at least not in the same way. They can borrow large sums of money because they are safer to lend to. Utilities have the ability to recoup justified operating costs directly from their ratepayers, and earn an assigned rate of return on invested capital.

For these reasons, they are a quasi-governmental entity. Governments, theoretically, can always raise taxes to cover operating expenses and incur heavy debt loads to, as examples, fund war efforts, deal with economic recessions, etc.

Regulated utilities are similar, with one key exception: The Public Utility Commission acts as the direct oversight body. Governments make laws, and therefore are the ultimate authority. In many ways, the utility and the PUC are like parents—they work together to grow the system and meet the needs of the region and communities.

Today, the opportunity and the challenge is to build a carbon-free electricity and transportation system that eliminates at least 60 percent of our contribution to carbon-induced climate change—*in twelve years!*

The regulated utility business model is designed and perfectly positioned for just such a challenge.

# EPILOGUE

The challenge is clear. The urgency is acute. The fastest way to a carbon-free electricity system is to combine a grassroots, bottom up consumer engagement strategy with a return to the state-level regulated utility business model and a national government policy that clearly states the objectives.

There is some chance that enough demand could be created with the Carbon IRA framework so that the carbon-free electricity infrastructure could be built primarily through private sector competition. But I'm a realist. I think the Carbon IRA is best suited for jump-starting consumer engagement, and for creating beta testers and early adopters.

YouTility, taken to its logical conclusion, essentially severs consumers from their utility for all but a small amount of emergency or backup power. In my wildest dream, I see the Carbon IRA & YouTility consumer engagement framework driving business in much the same way as internet, wireless, and cellular communications sectors drove digital platforms with minimum government intervention.

However, I often describe electricity as the foundation of our lifestyles and our economy. It's in the basement, in the walls, in the alley behind our house, and out in the country at some large power station—all connected by wires we don't notice.

Figure 29. From Wall Street traders to you and me, we stare at screens and rely on electricity all day, every day

Digital communications, on the other hand, are at the top of the economy. We stare at screens all day. You can't NOT notice them. We communicate with people 24/7/365 through these screens. Most of our work day is "screen to screen." Let's face it, most of our social activity is "screen to screen" these days.

The digital giants driving the economy today are customer-facing entities. I want to believe that utilities could also be true customer-facing entities. But I am older and wiser than I was when I wrote *Lights Out.*

Let me be clear: Including the regulated utility business model as the "third leg" of the stool is purely in the interest of speed—of building out the infrastructure on a schedule commensurate with the urgency of the threat. I think this approach comes the closest to a guaranteed, or assured, way to get to where we want to be when we want to get there.

But at the end of the day, I don't care how we get there. We just need to get there. Fast.

*The clock is ticking.*

# ACKNOWLEDGEMENTS

Gratitude goes to the folks who were willing to read and comment on early drafts of this book. The ideas you have just been exposed to came about after a long career in the electricity industry. It is impossible to acknowledge all the friends, colleagues, academics, engineers, managers, executives and even random acquaintances who shaped that career.

These ideas are also shaped by many avocational interests, such as my passion for systems concepts, history of technologies, and sociology. My partial work towards a higher degree in sociology, with a focus on financial engineering, helped me get smarter about macro-economics.

The six years Kristy (my spouse) and I published the newsletter, *Common Sense on Energy and Our Environment*, between 1990 and 1996, helped me understand the complexities of addressing environmental issues when you come at them without a pre-ordained ideology.

But what really made the ideas expressed here come alive were the dinner conversations I've had with Kristy and my two daughters, Amira and Elena (the illustrator), while they were in high school and college. Brainstorming with the next generation proved invaluable.

# ABOUT THE AUTHOR

Jason Makansi is the author of two electricity industry books, *Lights Out: The Electricity Crisis, the Global Economy, and What It Means To You* (John Wiley, 2007), and *An Investor's Guide to the Electricity Economy* (John Wiley, 2002), as well as hundreds of professional and academic articles. He was editor-in-chief of the leading professional journal on power plant engineering and has been active in the electricty-generation industry for nearly forty years.

As president of Pearl Street since 2001, an independent consulting firm focused on new technology deployment, he has been engaged by the largest electricity industry firms, electric utilities, garage-shop inventors, and investors.

In 2006, Makansi co-launched the Pearl Street Fund, investing in the electricity industry supply and delivery chain, and served as Director of Research for three years, and he functioned as executive director for two separate policy organizations focused on grid-scale energy storage.

He earned his BS degree in chemical engineering from Columbia University. Makansi has also published a novel, *The Moment Before*, and numerous short stories. He has been a sought-after speaker for audiences as large as 2,000, for small workshops, and for every size group in-between.

To invite Jason to speak to your organization on the potential and power of the Carbon IRA & YouTility framework, contact layladogpress@gmail.com.